Hayek and the Market

PLUTO PERSPECTIVES

Series Editor: Professor Robert Moore

Pluto Perspectives has created a forum for academics and commentators on the left of the ideological and political spectrum to offer sustained analytical critiques of individuals, institutions, themes and movements on what has now come to be identified as the 'New Right'

Forthcoming titles:

Philosophy and the New Right
TED BENTON

Citizenship and Social Class
T.H. MARSHALL
New Introduction by Tom Bottomore

The Political Involvement of the Christian Right in Southern Africa
PAUL GIFFORD

Hayek and the Market

Jim Tomlinson

Pluto Perspectives

PLUTO PRESS
London • Winchester, Mass

First published 1990 by Pluto Press
345 Archway Road, London N6 5AA
and 8 Winchester Place, Winchester
MA 01890, USA

Copyright © Jim Tomlinson 1990

All rights reserved

British Library Cataloguing in Publication Data
Tomlinson, Jim
  Hayek and the market.
  1. Economics. Theories
  I. Title
  330.1

ISBN 0-7453-0388-9

Library of Congress Cataloging in Publication Data
Tomlinson, Jim
  Hayek and the market / Jim Tomlinson
  p. cm. – (Pluto perspectives)
  Includes bibliographical references.
  ISBN 0-7453-0388-9
  ISBN 0-7453-0479-6 (pbk.)
  1. Hayek, Friedrich A. von (Friedrich August), 1899- . 2. Mixed economy. 3. Capitalism. 4. Socialism. I. Title. II. Series.
HB101.H39T66 1990
330.1–dc20   90-31491
                                                           CIP

Typeset by Stanford Desktop Publishing, Milton Keynes
Printed by Billing & Sons Ltd, Worcester

Contents

Works by Friedrich Hayek — vi

Acknowledgements — vii

Introduction — viii

1. A Biographical Overview — 1
2. Liberty, Democracy, Law and Justice — 17
3. Evolution, Reason and Morals — 43
4. Full Employment, Inflation, Welfare and Trade Unions — 67
5. Hayek and Socialism — 100
6. Conclusions: Hayek at the End of the Twentieth Century — 125

Bibliography — 152

Index — 160

Works by Friedrich Hayek are cited according to the following abbreviations:

Capitalism: *Capitalism and the Historians* (1954), London: Routledge & Kegan Paul.
Choice: *Choice in Currency* (1976), London: Institute of Economic Affairs. (Reprinted in *New Studies*, pp. 218–31.)
Collectivist: *Collectivist Economic Planning* (1935), London: Routledge & Kegan Paul.
Constitution: *The Constitution of Liberty* (1960), London: Routledge & Kegan Paul.
Counter-Revolution: *The Counter-Revolution of Science* (2nd edn 1979, originally published 1952), Chicago: Liberty Press.
Denationalisation: *The Denationalisation of Money* (2nd edn 1978), London: Institute of Economic Affairs.
Economic: *Economic Freedom and Representative Government* (1973), London: Institute of Economic Affairs. (Reprinted as Ch. 8 of *New Studies*.)
Fatal: *The Fatal Conceit: The Errors of Socialism: The Collected Works of F.A. Hayek*, vol. 1 (1988), London: Routledge.
Full Employment: *Full Employment at Any Price?* (1974), London: Institute of Economic Affairs. (A revised version of *New Studies*, pp. 197–209.)
Individualism: *Individualism and Economic Order* (1948), London: Routledge & Kegan Paul.
Law: *Law, Legislation and Liberty*, 3 vols (1973, 1976, 1979), London: Routledge & Kegan Paul.
Mill: *John Stuart Mill and Harriet Taylor: Their Friendship and Subsequent Marriage* (1951), London: Routledge & Kegan Paul.
Monetary: *Monetary Theory and the Trade Cycle* (1933), London: Jonathan Cape.
Nationalism: *Monetary Nationalism and International Stability* (1937), London: Longmans, Green & Co.
New Studies: *New Studies in Philosophy, Politics, Economics and the History of Ideas* (1978), London: Routledge & Kegan Paul.

Prices: *Prices and Production* (1931), London: Routledge & Kegan Paul.
Profits: *Profits, Interest and Investment* (1939), London: Routledge & Kegan Paul.
Pure Theory: *The Pure Theory of Capital* (1941), London: Routledge & Kegan Paul.
Road: *The Road to Serfdom* (1944), London: Routledge & Kegan Paul.
Sensory: *The Sensory Order: An Inquiry into the Foundations of Theoretical Psychology* (1952), London: Routledge & Kegan Paul.
Studies: *Studies in Philosophy, Politics and Economics* (1967), London: Routledge & Kegan Paul.
Three: *The Three Sources of Human Values* (1978), reprinted as an appendix in *Law*, vol. 3.
Tiger: *A Tiger by the Tail: The Keynesian Legacy of Inflation* (2nd edn 1978), London: Institute of Economic Affairs (ed by S.R. Shenoy).
Trend: 'The Trend of Economic Thinking' (1933), *Economica* vol. 13, no. 2, pp. 121-37.
Unemployment: *1980s Unemployment and the Unions* (1980), London: Institute of Economic Affairs.

A comprehensive bibliography of Hayek's writings up to 1985 is given in J. Gray, *Hayek on Liberty* (2nd edn 1986), Oxford: Blackwell.

Acknowledgements
In writing a book of this broad character I have been especially grateful for the help of others when touching upon their areas of expertise. Errors and misunderstandings have been reduced by the comments of my colleague Gillian Morris and by the discussion at the journal *Economy and Society* seminar on 'Democracy and the State', especially comments by Paul Hirst.
  I am once again extremely grateful to Mrs Christine Newnham for typing the manuscript with exemplary speed and efficiency.

Introduction

Friedrich Hayek has in recent years emerged as a central figure in what has come to be called the New Right. This short book is written in response to that emergence, and to the undoubted importance and influence of Hayek's writing. Hayek's writing is important because it is probably the most systematic attempt in the twentieth century to provide intellectual foundations for a system of private property, free markets and minimal government. Whilst Hayek draws explicitly on a wide range of previous authors, he offers not just a synthesis but also many developments of his own to the case for such an economic and social system.

Hayek's work cannot be easily categorised. It is a complex and possibly contradictory mixture of liberalism (in the European rather than the American sense) and conservatism. He is an advocate of liberalism in economic affairs – of free markets, very limited government held in check by entrenched constitutional powers, and pervasive hostility to post-war economic management, especially 'Keynesianism' – without however being an advocate of 'laissez-faire'. Indeed, one of the ways he attempts to go beyond what he calls the 'excesses' of nineteenth-century liberalism in this regard is to argue for a positive programme of reform in such areas as property law and law of contract in order to provide a more favourable environment for the operation of private property and markets.

Hayek is a conservative most obviously in his veneration of tradition, and in his belief that most of the forms of social organisation that exist in capitalist economies are the product of a long process of evolution. Thus private property is not something to be defended purely on intellectual or rational grounds, but also as the successful product of a process of evolutionary 'sifting' of institutions over the centuries. Hayek also tends to conservatism in social affairs, notably in his attitude to religion and the family, which means he fits uneasily into the libertarianism that is especially strong amongst the American New Right. (The tension in Hayek's work between his liberalism and his conservatism is further discussed in Chapter 3.)

Hayek, then, is an extremely learned writer, much of whose work is of an abstractness and difficulty which confine its audience to small numbers of fellow academics. Despite this, his work has increasingly been credited with having significantly influenced policy in several countries in the 1970s and 1980s. This recent influence has been built partly on the previous, more limited effects that some of his writing had achieved.

Hayek first came to something like popular notice in 1944 with his book *The Road to Serfdom*. This was particularly aimed at a British and, to a lesser extent, American audience. In both countries it was widely reviewed and discussed, and especially in the USA was an important contribution to the revival of intellectual conservatism, then in eclipse from the days of the New Deal (Nash, 1976, pp. 7–9, 13). If in Britain the response to this book was less enthusiastic, it was not insignificant, and seems, for example, to have been crucial in the eventual founding of the Institute of Economic Affairs (in 1957), which in later years was to be a major source for the propagation of Hayek's ideas (Burton, 1984, pp. xv–xxxii) and important in providing intellectual support for the Thatcher brand of conservatism. *The Road to Serfdom* seems to have excited altogether less interest in other parts of Europe, partly because it was very much aimed at a particular juncture in the political history of Britain (and the USA) a juncture which was rather different in almost all other European countries.

Hayek was to re-emerge in a significant way on the public

stage only many years later. But in the intervening period his theoretical works were undoubtedly influential (at least amongst some intellectuals) in many parts of the world. A token of this is that by the 1970s he had been awarded honorary doctorates from universities in Japan, Guatemala, Chile, Argentina and the USA, in addition to the highest academic honours in Britain, West Germany and Austria.

However, the real revival of Hayek's influence came in the 1970s with the break-up of the post-war consensus in many advanced capitalist countries. This influence was uneven. In West Germany it seems to have been limited because the broad development of German policy, unlike that of many other advanced capitalist countries, was to move from a more free-market to a more interventionist set of policies in these years (Barry, 1987, chs 1, 7). In other continental European countries also the impact was limited (though certainly not absent), partly because so much of Hayek's work related to an Anglo-Saxon intellectual milieu, and drew most of its examples from the British/American world where Hayek spent most of his working life. In France, for example, 'Les écrits de Friedrich Hayek, à l'exception sans doute de *La Route de la servitude*, sont peu connus du public francophone etant donne que la plupart d'entre eux et les études qui leur ont été consacrées ne sont accessibles qu'en anglais ou en allemand' (Dostaler and Ethier, 1989, p. 9).[1]

In addition, the USA and Britain offered political opportunities for policies congenial to Hayek's approach because of the almost simultaneous election of Thatcher and Reagan in, respectively, 1979 and 1980. Whilst neither of these election victories owed very much directly to the revival of New Right ideas, to some extent the ground was made more fertile for the new conservatism by such ideas. And in both countries Hayek was a major figure in that revival. (On the USA see, e.g., Peele 1984; on the UK, e.g., Gamble 1988.)

In Britain in 1981 Mrs Thatcher was to proclaim that 'I am a great admirer of Professor Hayek. Some of his books are absolutely supreme – *The Constitution of Liberty* and the three volumes of *Law, Legislation and Liberty* – and would well be read by almost every honourable member' (Hansard [Commons] 10 Feb 1981). By 1989 academic commentators were perceiving the influence of Hayek behind major parts of Conservative legislation – on industrial relations (Wedderburn, 1989) and on the poll tax (Leathers, 1989).

Whilst Hayek's importance and influence has often been recognised by his supporters and opponents, the number of reasonably detailed sceptical accounts of his work are strikingly few. Indeed the only book-length attempt by a socialist to criticise Hayek's work remains Wootton's *Freedom Under Planning* of 1945, written as a riposte to *The Road to Serfdom*.² There are very good, critical discussions of Hayek's work – notably Kukathas (1989), Gissurarson (1987), Gray (1984), Barry (1979) – but all of these start from a basic sympathy with liberalism.³

This book is written by a democratic socialist, and thus someone basically out of sympathy with Hayek's ideas. However, it is not a work of denigration, but of sceptical appraisal. It recognises the significance of Hayek's work, and recognises its attractions as a system of thought, but tries to maintain a critical distance.

The book, whilst written explicitly from a democratic socialist viewpoint, does not counterpose to Hayek another complete system of ideas. Partly this is due to sheer intellectual incapacity – to provide such a complete system would demand competences which I certainly do not possess. But, in addition, I would argue that socialism needs to be sceptical of the ambition of providing a complete 'alternative' world outlook. I would see it as a fundamental intellectual error by socialists to try to provide an hermetically sealed set of theories, wholly independent of non-socialist social and political thought. Rather, I would see the socialist task as one of critically engaging with the existing intellectual traditions from a position which holds to traditional socialist objectives – egalitarianism, democracy, co-operation, fraternity - but I do not believe the way to advance these objectives can be to stand 'outside' the main streams of Western thought.

This book is called *Hayek and the Market* because it is the concept of the market, and Hayek's advocacy of it as the key institution of a free society, that lies at the heart of his work. To make that point is not to try to reduce his arguments to a single thesis, which would be absurd. But the market does form a focus for many of Hayek's concerns – for his theory of knowledge, his theory of law and his political arguments – as well as for his more directly economic writings.

In addition, the concept of the market lies at the heart of Hayek's differences with socialism, and yet at the same time is the area where socialism seems currently most unsure of itself. Most obviously in Eastern Europe and the Soviet Union, we have in recent years seen a turn to 'market forces' which seem to be commonly portrayed by reformers in these countries in neoliberal or Hayekian terms. Equally, notions of the market have been central to the debates in Western Europe about the (clouded) future of socialism in those countries. Hence, to focus attention on Hayek's account of the market is both to highlight the key arguments of his work and at the same time to discuss those issues where his ideas seem currently most politically potent.

Notes

1. Interestingly, this book is a French-Canadian rather than French initiative.
2. H.E. Finer's *Road to Reaction* (1946), also written as a response to *The Road to Serfdom*, cannot be said to get to serious grips with Hayek's arguments.
3. Professor Meghnad Desai is preparing a substantial critical account of Hayek's economics writings.

1
A Biographical Overview

Friedrich August von Hayek was born in Vienna in 1899, the child of an academic family.[1] He served in the Austrian army during the First World War, and then studied at the University of Vienna, becoming a doctor of law in 1921 and a doctor of political science in 1925.

Beginning adult life as a 'mild Fabian', Hayek was soon influenced by the work of Austrian economists, notably Carl Menger (1840–1921), von Wieser (1851–1926) and von Mises (1881-1973), attending the seminars run by the last two of these in Vienna in the early 1920s. These men together may be seen as the founders of the Austrian school of economics, which ever since has formed a distinctive strand of economic theorising, distinct from the mainstream of neoclassical economics which has been dominant in most North American and Western European countries, but especially in the English-speaking world.[2] Hayek as an economic theorist owes much to this tradition, though he has developed his own distinctive positions within it.

In 1923–4 Hayek visited the USA. He found the theoretical level of discussion by economists there inferior to that in Vienna, American economists being largely concerned with practical issues rather than the methodological and theoretical concerns typical of the Austrian school. Hayek published work (in German) on US monetary policy, but his main concerns at this time were theoretical, and may be broadly defined as the monetary aspects of trade cycles, i.e. fluctuations in output and employment (essays from this period are in McCloughry, 1984).

From 1927 he was director of the Austrian Institute for Business Cycle Research, which he cofounded with von Mises, and from 1929 to 1931 he was also a lecturer in economics at Vienna University. Hayek's rise to prominence in English-language economics began when he was invited to lecture at the London School of Economics (LSE) in 1931. These lectures led to his appointment as Tooke Professor of Economic Science and Statistics at the LSE, after the post had been turned down by Hubert Henderson. Hayek was to retain this job until 1949, becoming a British citizen in 1938. The LSE lectures were published in 1931 as *Prices and Production*, and with that work Hayek became what Hicks (1967, p. ix) has called 'One of the chief contributors to that blaze of controversy' over monetary theory and policy in the 1930s.

Hayek's work followed shortly after the publication of Keynes's *Treatise on Money* (1930). Whilst both were works of high theory, they raised pressing practical issues relating to the great depression unfolding from 1929 onwards. The two works and responses to them formed the centrepiece of an academic controversy that was to rage in the major economic journals over a number of years.

Prices argued that the roots of slumps must be sought in excessive credit creations during the preceding economic expansions. Hayek argued that in the 1920s, market interest rates had fallen below the natural rate of interest, i.e. the long-run rate required to equate savings and investment. This had led to an excessive level of investment, above the level warranted by the level of savings, especially investment in fixed capital. Thus the structure of production had been distorted, with the consequence that eventually it would be restored to normality only by a slump. Kaldor, an economist at the LSE at the time, said that at the time of its publication *Prices* 'fascinated the academic world of economists by a new theory of industrial fluctuations which in theoretical conception, and perhaps even more in its practical implications, was diametrically opposed to the current trend of monetary thought' (1942, p. 359). The practical implications included the notion that as slump was a necessary correction of previous excesses, therefore it ought not to be countered by further distorting monetary expansions, or indeed by any demand-expanding measures, as advocated by Keynes and his associates. Hayek himself played little role in connecting his theory to current policy in Britain, though he was a co-signatory (along with L. Robbins, A. Plant and T.E. Gregory) to a letter in the London *Times* in October 1932 attacking Keynes's and other economists' support for expanding public expenditure to counteract the slump. However, in 1934 Lionel Robbins (also an economics professor at LSE) published his book *The Great Depression*, which used the Hayekian approach to offer a policy-orientated and anti-Keynesian analysis of the current slump. Robbins also advocated Hayekian-style analysis as a member of the Economic Advisory Council, a high-powered committee formed to advise the Prime Minister on economic policy.

Whilst the approach of *Prices* gained some immediate adherents, it was bitterly criticised by other economists, especially those from Cambridge. Keynes, responding to Hayek's review of his *Treatise*, wrote of Hayek's book, that it 'seems to me to be one of the most frightful muddles I have ever read, with scarcely a sound proposition in it beginning with p. 45, and yet it remains a book of some interest, which is likely to leave its mark on the mind of the reader. It is an extraordinary example of how, starting with a mistake, a remorseless logician can end up in Bedlam' (Keynes, 1931/1973, p. 252).

Piero Sraffa, another Cambridge economist who reviewed the book, said, 'From the beginning it is clear that a methodical criticism could not leave a brick standing in the logical structure built up by Dr. Hayek', and, further, that the book contained such 'a maze of contradictions [which] makes the reader so completely dizzy, that when he reaches the discussion of money he may out of despair be prepared to believe anything' (p. 45).

Subsequent assessments of *Prices* have tended to see it as

largely mistaken. Robbins, Hayek's greatest supporter in the 1930s, subsequently recanted that particular part of the legacy (Robbins, 1971, pp. 152–5). Hicks, a Nobel Laureate in economics and perhaps Britain's most important monetary theorist, wrote: 'That the immediate impact of the Hayek theory was extremely misleading is not now to be questioned; yet some of the issues to which he drew attention were real issues ...' (1967, p. 203). Whilst echoes of *Prices* are found in much of Hayek's later work, its approach had little long-run impact on most economists' analyses of economic fluctuations.

It would not be much of an exaggeration to say that the theoretical (but not policy) response to the slump was a fight between the positions of Hayek and Keynes. In the 1930s this battle was clearly lost by Hayek, and the Keynesians came to dominate the agenda of theoretical economics, especially in the English-speaking world. Hayek was later to regret not having fought harder against Keynes's *General Theory* around the time of its publication in 1936. As in the debates over the *Treatise*, 'I feared that before I had completed my analysis he would again have changed his mind' (*New Studies*, p. 284). In later years Hayek was to blame Keynes for many of the inflationary ills of the British and other Western economies, and, outliving Keynes (who died in 1946), he was able to argue by the 1970s that the 'Keynesian' post-war consensus had ended, as he had predicted, in rapid inflation and mass unemployment (*Tiger*). For Hayek, Keynes's *General Theory* was no such thing, but a tract for the times, born of the passing needs of policy. It led to the 'final disaster', the idea that unemployment is the responsibility of governments (*Unemployment*, p. 57).

Hayek's view of Keynes's work is imbued with a strong moralism. Whilst personal relations seem to have been largely amicable (and Keynes commented particularly favourably on *The Road to Serfdom* – Keynes, 1945/1980, pp. 385–8), Hayek over time increasingly portrayed Keynes's economic arguments as a result of his moral deficiency as well as his lack of theoretical sophistication (*New Studies*, ch. 18; *Fatal*, chs. 4, 5).³ This culminated in Hayek's bizarre statement that 'only a confessed immoralist could indeed defend measures of policy on the grounds that "in the long run we are all dead". For the only groups to have spread and developed are those among whom it became customary to try to provide for children and later descendants whom one might never see' (*Fatal*, p. 84). This is linked to a grotesque misrepresentation of Keynes's views, in which his famous phrase about the long run is said to mean 'it does not matter what long-range damage we do; it is the present moment alone, the short-run – consisting of public opinion, demands, votes, and all the stuff and bribes of demagoguery – which count' (*Fatal*, p. 57). *as against Marx*

In fact the meaning Keynes attached to this phrase was quite different – it was a criticism of economists who when faced with an economic crisis made do with the comment that in the long-run economic forces would tend back to equilibrium. Not unreasonably, Keynes saw such views as a dereliction of duty. 'Economists set themselves too easy, too useless a task if in tempestuous seasons they only tell us that when the storm is long past the ocean is flat again' (Keynes, 1923/1971, p. 65).

Hayek continued to work in the highly technical area of trade-cycle theory after 1931, publishing a revised version of *Prices* in 1935, and two related books, *Monetary Theory and the Trade Cycle* (which had appeared in German in 1929) in 1933, and *Profits, Interest and Investment* in 1939. A central part of Hayek's theory in this period was what he called the 'Ricardo Effect'. This meant that in a boom the rising demand for consumer goods drives up their prices, leading to a fall in real wages. This, in turn, leads to an increase in investment demand, but (and this is the crucial point) this is coupled with and eventually offset by a fall in capital: output ratios as real wages fall. Hayek thus argued (contrary to other trade-cycle theorists) that investment will tail-off in a slump even though profits are rising.

Again, such a position was bound to raise the ire of Keynesian economists, who stressed the effects of low profit expectations in reducing investment levels as crucial to slumps. Kaldor (1939, 1942) published savage attacks on Hayek's position, though in general by the late 1930s the Keynesians dominated the theoretical agenda in this area. Hayek himself moved away from a focus on monetary theory to a concern with capital theory, publishing in 1941 *The Pure Theory of Capital*, which may be seen as his last major work in pure economic theory. In it he attempted to extend the Austrian school theory of capital, 'to develop the most austere and stringent abstract model of the role of time-lapse within a productive technology' (Shackle 1981, p. 245). Views as to the significance of the work differ. Blaug, in a standard work on the history of economic thought, remarks that 'Hayek's *Pure Theory* was poorly received ... and suffers from imprecision at critical turning points in the argument. But it contains many valuable flashes' (1985, p. 572). On the other hand, adherents of Austrian school economics suggest the book 'contains some of the most penetrating thoughts on the subject that have ever been published' (Machlup, 1974, p. 509). Even other sympathisers, whilst recognising the major intellectual feat, have questioned where *The Pure Theory* was going, especially as Hayek's approach ruled out any statistical or practical 'operationalisation' of the theory (Shackle, 1981, p. 250). Outside the (very limited) field of capital theory, Hayek's book had limited impact and had few links with either the contemporary concerns of economists or the public at large.

Even before *The Pure Theory* Hayek had published major work which heralded his movement from highly abstract economic theory into much wider issues of philosophy and social theory, work on which was laid the foundation for much of his reputation outside the narrow world of theoretical economists.

In his inaugural lecture at the LSE in 1933 Hayek linked his version of trade-cycle theory to broader issues of economic organisation, and explicitly stated his adherence to the policy tenets of the classical economists 'whose presumption against government interference sprang from a wide range of demonstrations that isolated acts of interference definitely frustrated the attainment of those ends which all accepted as desirable' (*Trend*, p. 124). In the same lecture he proclaimed his commitment, not to 'laissez-faire' but to a very narrow range of government interventions in the economy. This, he argued, was because of the *intellectual* error of socialism, which failed to understand that economic activity is not 'anarchic' but co-ordinated, but that co-ordination is not by deliberate planning, but from the workings of 'spontaneous institutions'. All advocates of economic planning were labelled socialists, and thus it followed: 'In this sense there are, of course, very few people left who are not socialists' (p. 135).

It would not be a great exaggeration to say that the agenda of issues Hayek was to spend most of the rest of his life working on was raised in this 1933 article. Most striking is the commitment to exposing the intellectual errors and conceit of socialism in its claim to be able to plan society rationally to function in a superior manner to a free market. The desire to expose and destroy the intellectual basis of socialism (in this very broad sense) may be seen as the driving force behind most of Hayek's work down to and very much including *The Fatal Conceit* of 1988.

Initially, in the 1930s, this intellectual criticism of socialism focused quite narrowly on the issue of economic planning as an allocative device. In the collection edited by Hayek in 1935, *Collectivist Economic Planning*, Hayek outlined the arguments which had been made over the previous decades against the possibility of a rational socialism. This essentially came down to a critique of any central determination of the pattern of output, because such centralisation would be unable either to obtain or to co-ordinate and deploy the mountainous quantities of information needed to react to changes in consumer tastes and production techniques. 'It is this formal aspect, this fact that one central authority has to solve the economic problem of distributing a limited amount of resources between a practically infinite number of competing purposes, that constitutes the problem of socialism as a method' (*Collectivist*, pp. 16-17).

Hayek goes on to discuss various solutions to this problem, including a socialist economy made up of competing but collectively owned enterprises, but argues that in this case the absence of private property rights in such enterprises would lead to an absence of risk-taking which would be fatal to improvements in productivity. Along the way he castigates other 'intermediate' attempts to plan economies, essentially arguing that only a fully market economy can effectively use to rational effect the enormous diversity of knowledge available to consumers and producers.

This issue of the relation between knowledge and economic activity was taken up in a key article in 1937 entitled *Economics and Knowledge* (reprinted in *Individualism*, ch. 2). Many years later Hayek was to see this paper as crucial in his development from a 'very pure and narrow economic theorist' to focus on 'questions usually regarded as philosophical' (*Studies*, p. 91).

Why was this article so important for Hayek? In summary terms the answer is that it brought out the limitations of traditional neoclassical economic theory, limitations he was particularly sensitive to because of their links to his analysis of the irrationality of socialism (Caldwell, 1988). Hayek's article brought out some of the problems of the traditional economists' notion of an economy tending to equilibrium. He argued that for this to be empirically meaningful it required that the *knowledge* of economic agents be co-ordinated; otherwise those agents' different expectations about the world might lead to divergence rather than convergence of behaviour. Hayek wanted to hang on to the notion of equilibrium, whilst at the same time stressing the inherently *subjective* nature of the knowledge of economic agents. Hayek attempts to maintain both his belief in equilibrium and the subjectivity of economic knowledge by suggesting that markets feed back into that economic knowledge, leading to individuals' plans being made compatible.

This does not seem a very satisfactory solution, as it supposes a feedback only from the state of the world to agents' expectations, whilst ignoring the impact of agents' expectations on that world (Caldwell, 1988, p. 529). But in the current context the important point is not the plausibility of Hayek's argument but how it links to his life's work of criticising socialism. The connection is clear in a review he wrote in 1940, 'Socialist Calculation: The Competitive "Solution"', commenting on the work of socialist economists who, in turn, were responding to the kind of arguments in *Collectivist*. (This article is included in *Individualism*, Ch. 9.)

In essence, these socialist economists argued that an economically perfectly rational socialism was possible as long as the central planners mimicked the decision rules of a capitalist system. Crucially this means pricing products equal to marginal cost, a rule which, it was argued, could be imposed on socialist enterprise managers just as the market imposes it on capitalist entrepreneurs. Hayek's response was not to attack the theoretical aspect of this argument but its practicability:

> There is of course, no logical impossibility of conceiving a directing organ of the collective economy which is not only 'omnipresent and omniscient' as Dickinson conceives it, but also omnipotent and which therefore would be in a position to change without delay every price by just the amount that is required. When, however, one proceeds to consider the actual apparatus by which this sort of adjustment is to be brought about, one begins to wonder whether anyone should really be prepared to suggest that, within the domain of practical possibility such a system will even distantly approach the efficiency of a system where the required changes are brought about by the spontaneous actions of the persons immediately concerned (*Individualism*, p. 187).

(These issues are discussed further in Chapter 5.)

This paragraph marks Hayek's growing divergence from traditional economic theory, because the socialist economists had used that theory to make what he considered a wholly absurd case for socialism. That they had been able to do so reflected above all that theory's inadequate conception of the subjective and particular character of the knowledge of economic agents. More broadly, Hayek believed economics had not sufficiently examined the conditions for what he was later to call the 'spontaneous order' which emerged from individuals acting on their individual and particular knowledge.

These concerns defined the agenda for much of Hayek's subsequent work. Within his (almost) life-long concern to attack socialism, the focus was to be on the acquisition and use of knowledge, and, on the other hand, the very broad conditions which underlie a spontaneous, market order. The concern with the conditions and character of knowledge led to a series of papers attacking what Hayek called 'scientism', the belief that the methods of the social sciences could and should ape those of the natural sciences. In a series of articles in the early 1940s (later published in *The Counter-Revolution of Science*) the attack was on the way in which, Hayek alleged, many of the mistaken theories of society (including socialism) were grounded on such notions of the human capacity to understand.

Hayek, under the influence of Karl Popper, especially his *Logic of Scientific Discovery*, later shifted his ground on the relation between the methods of the natural and social sciences. He came to accept that both should be based on attempts to refute hypotheses (Preface to *Studies*). But he retained a belief in the inescapably limited nature of human knowledge of society, which would seem to owe much to Kant (Gray, 1984, ch. 1), and hence the inappropriateness of trying to reconstruct society as if such knowledge existed.

This abstract and historical work, carried out in the early years of the war, was followed in 1944 by the publication of what probably remains Hayek's best-known book, *The Road to Serfdom*. This was, as Hayek states quite clearly in his preface, a political book, attacking the trend of economic policy towards socialism, especially in Britain. He envisages

Britain going down the road of Germany at the end of the First World War by drawing the wrong lessons from the wartime economy. The central object of his criticism (and for most purposes this is, for Hayek, synonymous with socialism) is economic planning in the sense of centralised direction of the economy. The root problem is that such economic planning must attempt the impossible task of centralising all economic knowledge; pursuit of this objective will require more and more authoritarian powers for government, and hence, if pursued, will inevitably end in the suppression of liberty exactly as it had in Germany and Russia. For Hayek democratic socialism is a contradiction in terms, but its errors are not limited to those who call themselves socialists – Hayek's book is dedicated to 'The Socialists of All Parties', and he sees his argument as very much going against the tide of the time.

The Road found a wide public in Britain and the USA, being given the accolade of a Reader's Digest condensation in North America. Similar political concerns led Hayek to play the key role in the founding of the Mont Pelerin society, a group of like-minded liberals who met periodically after the founding conference in Switzerland in 1947. Their basic aims were to rebuild the intellectual foundations of a free society, which Hayek and his collaborators felt had been lost sight of by the 1940s. (Hayek's address to the founding conference is in *Studies*, ch. 10.)

In 1950 Hayek moved from London to the University of Chicago, as a professor of social and moral sciences. The University of Chicago had a growing reputation as a centre of liberal economics, and perhaps appeared more congenial than British academic life, where such liberalism was very much a minority view.

In 1951 Hayek published his most curious book, *John Stuart Mill and Harriet Taylor: Their Friendship and Subsequent Marriage*. This is a very scholarly account of the relationship between one of Hayek's intellectual 'heroes' and the woman with whom he conducted an affair, and subsequently married after her husband's death. The curious feature of the book is that its explicit rationale is to show how Harriet Taylor was substantially responsible for Mill's movement from the pure stream of liberalism (as shown notably, of course, in *On 'Liberty'* [see ch. 2 below]) to his avowal of a form of socialism in later editions of his *Political Economy*. Hayek's book thus appears as a highly intellectual version of 'cherchez la femme'.

On a completely different plane is Hayek's 1952 book, *The Sensory Order*, a book on theoretical psychology and its philosophical underpinnings. This returned to (unpublished) work Hayek had done originally in the early 1920s. Whilst in its topic clearly separate from the rest of Hayek's writings, this book does share many of the philosophical assumptions of those writings. In particular, Hayek's Kantian scepticism about our ability to know 'how things really are in the world' is evident, and the related notion that the only aim of any science can be the development of a system of categories, organised on a deductive basis, which is adequate to the experience it seeks to order. Thus there is a clear continuity between this psychological theory about how knowledge is acquired and the stress on the limits of reason which has played such an important part in his attack on socialism.

A central aspect of Hayek's epistemology is its denial of knowledge as based on sense experience, and its emphasis on the importance of theory. Apart from its general implications for Hayek's work, one 'practical' consequence of this emphasis is its stress on theoretical training in universities. In his inaugural address at Freiburg University he was to tell the students: 'The chief gain from your study at the university must be an understanding of theory, and it is the only profit which you can gain nowhere else' (*Studies*, p. 266).

Until 1962 Hayek remained at Chicago. Whilst in the USA he retained close contact with events in Britain, playing a role in the foundation of the Institute of Economic Affairs in 1957, which was to provide a major vehicle for the dissemination of his ideas in Britain. He wrote on a number of topics in this period, including some highly political pieces on the current US economy (*Studies*, Part III). But the main product of this period is undoubtedly *The Constitution of Liberty* (1960), which is his single most important work. The purpose of the book is to restate the 'ideal of freedom which inspired modern Western civilisation', a restatement required by the fact that 'for almost a century the basic principles on which this civilisation was built have been falling into increasing disregard and oblivion' (*Constitution*, pp. 1–2). Much of the book, as might be expected from such a project, is highly theoretical and philosophical. There is also a substantial discussion of the institutions of liberty, which, for Hayek, means particularly legal institutions. But the final part of the book deals with a number of topical issues, such as the welfare state, trade unions, taxation and monetary policy, which embodied the kind of problem he believed crucial to the advance and retreat of freedom. The underlying theme of the book, if its 400-odd pages can be summarised in one sentence, is that there has been an *intellectual* failure to understand the conditions of liberty, and this has greatly facilitated the erosion of those conditions, an erosion which Hayek believes has gone very far in much of the West.

In 1962 Hayek moved from Chicago to become professor of economic policy at the University of Freiburg in West Germany, retiring and becoming professor emeritus in 1969. He became an honorary professor at the University of Salzburg in Austria, and among many academic honours was awarded the Nobel Prize for economics in 1974, jointly with the leftish Swedish economist Gunnar Myrdal. For both, the award of the prize was 'for their pioneering work in the theory of money and economic fluctuations and for their penetrating analysis of the interdependence of economic, social and institutional phenomena' (cited Machlup, 1977, p. xv).

In a speech following the award, Hayek congratulated the Nobel Prize committee on being willing to award the prize to someone 'whose views are as unfashionable as mine are' (Machlup, 1977, p. xvii). But the tide was already turning.

The 1970s saw an economic crisis in the West, accompanied by an intellectual crisis in the Keynesian-social democratic consensus Hayek had always anathematised. In that decade Hayek was not only to complete the three volumes of *Law, Legislation and Liberty* (1973, 1976 and 1979) which essentially developed the middle part of *The Constitution*, but also to participate in the great political debates of the time, notably on inflation, unemployment and trade unions. (Hayek returned to Freiburg in 1977.)

On inflation, Hayek continued his long-standing hostility to Keynesian policies, which, he believed, had been based on a misunderstanding of the causes of unemployment, and which had inevitably led to inflation. Thus, like many on the Right in these years, Hayek treated much of the economic crisis of the 1970s as a (long-delayed) demonstration of the errors of Keynesianism (*Tiger*).

Hayek's own analysis of unemployment remained very much the same as in the 1930s – it was the consequence of the preceding inflation, and the distortions of production thereby induced (*Full Employment at Any Price?*). Also very much in line with conservative British prejudices at the time was his hostility to trade unions, which he saw as the centrepiece of Britain's relative decline: 'All I can say with conviction is that, so long as general opinion makes it politically impossible to deprive the trade unions of their coercive powers, an economic recovery of Great Britain is also impossible' (*1980s Unemployment and the Unions*, p. 64).

But more startling products of this period were Hayek's proposals on the constitution and on money. On the constitution, a long-standing desire was to limit the capacities of majority governments by constitutional provision. This problem, in Hayek's view, became all the more urgent in the 1970s, when he linked the current economic crisis of high inflation and high unemployment to the political framework (*Economic Freedom and Representative Government*). In similar vein, in the third volume of *Law* (ch. 17), he proposed that a new second legislative chamber be established to determine the constitutional framework, what Hayek called the rules of conduct (including those of the lower house), based on an election by all 45-year-olds, who would choose from their number those to make up this body. Those elected would serve for 15 years, and be guaranteed public employment on retirement to insulate them from the pressures of private interest groups.

Perhaps even more radical was Hayek's proposal for the 'denationalisation' of money. He argued that the only foolproof method of preventing the decline in the value of money (i.e. inflation) was to allow competition in moneys, which would obviously require the ending of the state monopoly of its issue. Thus the logic of the market would be used to end government-induced debasement of the currency (*Denationalisation of Money*, 2nd edn, 1978; *Choice in Currency*, 1976). Whilst neither of these proposals has ever looked likely to be enacted, in Britain the enthusiasm amongst members of the Thatcher government for his general posture was shown by his award of the Companion of Honour in 1984.

Whilst the events of the 1970s provided a new opportunity for Hayek's views on topical matters to be widely disseminated, in the 1980s he has continued to work on broad issues of philosophy and social theory. In 1988 he published *The Fatal Conceit: The Errors of Socialism*. This had been planned as Hayek's contribution to his planned intellectual 'showdown' with socialism, an event which, however, never took place. The theme of the book is the grand dichotomy which underlies so much of Hayek's work:

> The main point of my argument is, then, that the conflict between, on the one hand, advocates of the spontaneous extended human order created by a competitive market, and on the other hand those who demand a deliberate arrangement of human interaction by central authority based on collective command over available resources is due to a factual error by the latter about how knowledge of these resources is and can be generated and utilised (*Fatal*, p. 7).

Notes

1. For more detailed biographical information see the Biographical Introductions to Nishiyama and Leube (1984) and Machlup (1979).
2. For an overview of Austrian school economics, see Hutchison (1981), ch. 7, or, in more detail, Shand (1984). For the historical background of Vienna in the 1920s, which Hayek accepts was very important in shaping his views (*Constitution*, p. viii), see Polanyi-Levitt and Mendell (1989).
3. Keynes was bisexual and an adherent of notions of 'the good life' which are in sharp contrast to Hayek's rather strait-laced moral stance. (On this aspect of Keynes, see Skidelsky 1983, chs 2, 6.)

2

Liberty, Democracy, Law and Justice

Hayek's work presents a complex and wide-ranging set of arguments which do not fit readily into the traditional categories of 'disciplines' in the human sciences. Yet these arguments are far from being a random, unconnected series of positions. Rather, they are united by being part of an enormously ambitious, and ultimately political, project, which can be summarised as the rebuilding of the foundations of traditional liberalism.

Liberalism is a word with many connotations, but the liberal tradition Hayek places himself in is a fairly specific one. It is a tradition which above all places its political priority on human *liberty* or *freedom*, where those words are used synonymously to mean freedom from the arbitrary will of other people. This, in turn, generates the argument that to sustain that liberty requires each person to have their own private domain of action, free from unwarranted interference by others acting individually or collectively, and, especially, free from coercion by the state.

Hayek argues that such a private domain requires the institution of private property, freedom of contract, and freedom of choice of employment. It also requires clear limits on democracy, in the sense of the right of majorities to pass laws to violate that private domain. Legislators, like citizens, therefore need to work within a framework of laws which are above and beyond those passed by legislatures; there must be a transcendent body of law which must be concerned with abstract rules of conduct, *not* with specific ends. When this is realised, law, not people, will rule; there will be the rule of law.

Finally, injustice in this framework is when that private domain is violated. Justice relates only to actions willed by people (individually or collectively); the term cannot be used to describe a state of affairs not intended by anyone. Hence Hayek bitterly attacks the notion of *social* justice, which, he argues, leads to illegitimate attacks on the distribution of material rewards generated by the market. This notion is doubly wrong. It uses the term *justice* inappropriately, because the distribution of those rewards is, by definition, neither just nor unjust, not being the result of anyone's intentions. Worse, the inappropriate use of justice as a category in this context leads to real injustice, as governments intervene in individuals' private domains to correct perceived injustices.

Hence notions of freedom, democracy, law and justice can be said to summarise Hayek's social and political philosophy. This chapter will look at each of these concepts in turn, outlining Hayek's positions and some of the difficulties these raise.

Liberty

Liberty is at the centre of Hayek's work. His most important work is called *The Constitution of Liberty*; his most famous, *The Road to Serfdom*, is concerned with the alleged threat to liberty. Hayek's definition of liberty is an essentially negative one – it is concerned with the absence of restraint on human thought and action, *not* the capacity to achieve any particular ends (*Constitution*, ch. 1). As in so much of Hayek's political philosophy, this view is grounded on an epistemology, a theory of knowledge that stresses human ignorance, and therefore the desirability of allowing scope for the unpredictable and unforeseeable. 'The case for individual freedom rests chiefly on the recognition of the inevitable ignorance of all of us concerning a great many of the factors on which the achievement of our ends and welfare depends' (*Constitution*, p. 29).

On the subject of liberty, as elsewhere, Hayek both builds on but partially rejects the legacy of John Stuart Mill. In *On 'Liberty'* (1859/1962) Mill based much of his case for freedom on the human tendency to error, but at the same time he saw the possibility of a straightforward rule to prevent incursions into that liberty. Mill (1859/1962, ch. 4) thought that liberty could be protected by making unacceptable any interference in a person's actions which affect only that person and no other. This may be called the 'classic' liberal position. But, Hayek argues, such a distinction is not very useful, as there are hardly any actions which may not affect others to some degree. For Hayek the key consideration is rather the expectations of people; for liberty there must be a protected domain where we can be reasonably sure our expectations will be realised, so that we can ground our choice of action on reliable data (*Constitution*, p. 145). So whilst Hayek is opposed to intervention in (im)moral conduct which affects no one but the doer (*Law*, vol. II, p. 101), his emphasis is on establishing an abstract set of rules of conduct which will establish this protected domain. These rules are abstract because they do not relate to particular purposes, but allow people to pursue their own ends, subject to rules which admit of no exception and therefore of no room for arbitrary action. They apply to the government as well as the governed.

These rules are *not* on a par with the menus of rights or freedoms we commonly see produced in bills of rights e.g. freedom of thought, speech, etc. (*Constitution*, p. 155). For Hayek, the danger of these lists of specific freedoms is that they will be seen as inclusive, excluding other freedoms which might become desirable as circumstances change (*Law*, vol. III, pp. 109–10). However, he is not opposed to such rights and freedoms having a statutory base as a tactical device to enlarge the scope of freedom, if they do not pretend to have this inclusive character.

Hayek emphasises that freedom must be freedom of action as well as of thought (*Constitution*, p. 33). Thus the emphasis on freedom requires that people exist in an institutional context which allows this freedom of action. For Hayek, this freedom of action requires freedom of choice of employment, but above all it requires the freedom to own and dispose of property. Not that everyone needs to own property to be free. The crucial point is that there be dispersed property ownership and therefore not a single employer of labour.

Whilst Hayek accepts the need for some coercion to maintain the conditions of freedom (*Constitution*, p. 21), his primary concern is the maintenance of a private domain where individuals may pursue their own ends. As already noted, this is based on a certain epistemological argument about the limits of knowledge, and the way in which knowledge is generated by individuals coping with the very specific circumstances they encounter. Equally, Hayek sees this freedom as generating morality, and hence as a key to the development of a sustainable 'spontaneous order'. These particular issues are returned to in Chapter 3. The important point here is that this definition of freedom logically leads to the view that the threat to freedom comes from any attempt to impose designs which block individual choice of action.

> Nobody with open eyes can any longer doubt that the danger to personal freedom comes chiefly from the Left, not because of any particular ideals it pursues, but because the various socialist movements are the only large organised bodies which, for aims which appeal to many, want to impose upon society a preconceived design (*Law*, vol. III, p. 129).

Hayek sits clearly in the liberal tradition in defining freedom in a 'negative' manner. A common alternative approach is to define freedom 'positively' as a capacity to attain certain ends. But if this is done liberty tends to lose all its specificity as a desirable objective, and becomes swallowed up in other goals. Rather than pursue this path of criticism of Hayek, it seems more fruitful to focus on (a) the content and (b) the status of liberty, defining liberty negatively, as Hayek does.

In content, Hayek's definition of liberty is ultimately 'quantitative'. He has no notion of absolute liberty; the issue is how many things can be done:

> That one should be allowed to do specific things is not liberty, though it may be called a 'liberty'; and while liberty is compatible with not being allowed to do specific things, it does not exist if one needs permission *for most of what one can do*. The difference between liberty and liberties is that which exists between a condition in which all is permitted that is not prohibited by general rules and one in which all is prohibited that is not explicitly permitted (*Constitution*, p. 19; emphasis added).

This passage seems to be a direct reply to Wootton's (1945) critical discussion of Hayek's *Road to Serfdom*, a discussion which remains one of the best on Hayek's arguments on freedom. Wootton suggested that freedom and liberty are best seen as always consisting of a conglomeration of freedoms and liberties, that there is no good reason to suppose that these different freedoms would be strengthened or eroded together, and that their compatibility with different states of social organisation was an *empirical* matter, not one to be decided from first principles. Writing in 1945, she was able to show how little most freedoms had, in fact, been eroded under planning in Britain, despite Hayek's pronouncements. The empirical relation between liberties and more recent history is taken up in Chapter 5, but the important point here is to register how much Hayek's argument evades Wootton's challenge by defining liberty only in the abstract. Nowhere does he attempt to draw up an alternative 'balance sheet' of liberties to that proposed by Wootton.

For Hayek, liberty is the only really important political value. (The only other significant one is democracy, which is returned to below.) This priority is explicable given the consequences he alleges to derive from the absence or presence of freedom. For him, progress towards civilisation has been the (unintended) consequence of freedom; the regression he perceives in Western societies since the late nineteenth century, the consequence of the erosion of that freedom. This grand historical schema is analysed in Chapter 3 below, but the point here is to register how far the whole edifice of Hayek's ideas rests on claims for the effects of freedom.

Some modern socialists have attempted to refute Hayek on his own ground, by agreeing with him that liberty is the crucial political value, but that it can only be realised by the institutions of democratic socialism, not by Hayek's liberal capitalism. But, as with the discussion of negative versus positive liberty, the danger here is that liberty will lose all its specificity as a political objective, and become a vague synonym for all that we find politically desirable. (This issue is discussed further in the concluding chapter of this book.)

Instead of this approach, it seems more helpful to question whether liberty (in Hayek's sense) really is such an overriding consideration. For Hayek, that status rests not only on arguments about the effects of liberty, but also on an explicit hostility to other political values, notably those of the Left. Of these, the focus of hostile attention is equality or egalitarianism, but equally condemned are cooperation and altruism extending beyond the level of immediate associates.

Hayek's hostility to these concerns is linked to his idea that market capitalism forms a 'spontaneous order', not a product of human design, in which markets impose order on life by allowing individuals freedom to use their own knowledge in pursuit of their own objectives. Like Adam Smith's invisible hand, this structure translates a pattern of individuals' pursuit of their own ends into a sustainable social order, as long as it is not disrupted by overextended government.

The pursuit of equality disrupts this order by attempting to impose a different system of valuation. In a market system, each person is rewarded by their contribution to the welfare of others. The pursuit of equality leads to attempts to apply a measure of *merit* to individuals' rewards. This cuts across the spontaneous order, as governments attempt the impossible, i.e. finding and then imposing a scale of merit agreeable to all. Their attempts to do so, Hayek argues, can only lead to growing coercion.

In similar vein, competition, not co-operation, is the lifeblood of the spontaneous order, the generator of progress in conditions where there is an absence of general agreement on ends to pursue co-operatively. Similarly, altruism is appropriate in small groups of individuals, but inappropriate in larger units, in 'society', where the spontaneous order is disrupted if individuals attempt *deliberately* to help others, rather than to allow the market to turn self-regarding actions to the benefit of all. Here Hayek draws on ideas expressed by Adam Smith, famously encapsulated in the quotation, 'By directing that industry in such a manner as its produce may be of the greatest value, he intends only his own gain, and he is in this, as in many other cases, led by an invisible hand to promote an end which was no part of his intention' (Smith, 1776/1976, IV, ii, 9, p. 456).

This summary of the basis of Hayek's hostility to traditional democratic socialist political objectives takes us to the foundation of his whole edifice of arguments. These arguments cannot all be commented on in the compass of this chapter. But let it suffice at this point to note the extent to which this edifice rests on a dichotomy: *either* a spontaneous order *or* the stark alternative of a descent into chaos. So, ultimately, Hayek's arguments rest on perceiving societies as principles in action – either the principle of the 'spontaneous order', or the 'socialist' principle of imposing human design. To this, one can counterpoise the view that societies are not organised around principles, but always consist of agglomerations of institutions which are contingently related. Political forces may attempt to impose certain objectives on these institutions, but they will always 'escape' such a single-ended project. Even more will the agglomeration of institutions escape such an imposition of a single principle. (This point is returned to in the final chapter, in discussing 'the market' and 'the plan' as societal principles.)

In this view, liberty (or liberties) becomes one objective alongside others (equality/inequality, competition/co-operation, altruism/self-regard), the relations between these sometimes being competitive, sometimes complementary, and here an almost infinite set of possible combinations of outcomes of attempts to attain these principles is possible. This view is developed further in the concluding chapter.

Returning to the question of liberty, the final general issue which arises is that of its conditions. Hayek takes the classic liberal position that private property (and this, crucially, includes the means of production) is central to liberty. The grounds for this position are the belief that such property is a necessary condition for the existence of that private domain which is, in turn, the core requirement for liberty. What is crucial about that domain is that it frees people from coercion by others. But the argument is not that everyone must become a self-employed capitalist to be free. Hayek is quite clear that what matters is the 'severalness' of property, and Hayek's argument here is worth quoting at length.

> In modern society, however, the essential requisite for the protection of the individual against coercion is not that he possess property but that the material means which enable him to pursue any plan of action should not be all in the exclusive control of one other agent. It is one of the accomplishments of modern society that freedom may be enjoyed by a person with practically no property of his own (beyond personal belongings like clothing – and even these can be rented out) and that we can leave the care of the property that serves our needs largely to others. The important point is that the property should be sufficiently dispersed so that the individual is not dependent on particular persons who alone can provide him with what he needs or who alone can employ him (*Constitution*, pp. 140-1).

This argument against the political consequences of a single employer is a compelling one. Hayek cites Trotsky's stark summary of the point: 'In a country where the sole employer is the State, opposition means death by slow starvation. The old principle, who does not work should not eat, has been replaced by a new one: who does not obey shall not eat' (cited *Constitution*, p. 137). But whilst this argument may be compelling against proposals for centralised state ownership of all the means of production, it cannot function as an argument in favour of traditional systems of private property. Severalty of property can be attained in a number of ways, by all different kinds and combinations of enterprise forms – co-operatives, state enterprises, self-employment, incorporated firms where the firm itself owns the enterprise's assets, and 'pure' private property where individual property owners own and control productive assets. Such structures, which are at the centre of debate in democratic socialism, are immune to Hayek's attacks on the grounds of their effects on liberty. (But he is hostile to, for example, co-operatives on economic grounds – an issue returned to in Chapter 5.)

Democracy

If Hayek is a classical liberal in the priority he accords to liberty, he is in the mainstream of conservative political thought in his scepticism about the virtues of democracy (i.e. majority rule): 'Not only peace, justice and liberty but also democracy is basically a negative value, a procedural rule which serves as a protection against despotism and tyranny, and certainly no more but not much less important than the first Three Great Negatives – or, to put it differently, a convention which mainly serves to prevent harm' (*Law*, vol. III, p. 133). Elsewhere (*Constitution*, p. 107) the case for democracy is expanded – as a way of resolving differences peacefully, as likely (but definitely not certain) to produce liberty, and as a means of educating the majority. But in all of these democracy is clearly a means, not an end in itself.

Democracy is to be clearly distinguished from liberty. The opposite of liberty is totalitarianism; the opposite of democracy is authoritarianism. Theoretically, authoritarian governments could act on liberal principles, i.e. by not intruding excessively into private domains (*Constitution*, pp. 103–4). Furthermore, there is a strong danger that democracy will subvert liberty, by allowing the majority of citizens to grant untrammelled powers to government to coerce individuals. So democracy is acceptable only in so far as it is coupled with limited government. Logically, these limits must stand outside majority determination; otherwise they could be changed by majority vote:

> The liberal regards it as important that the powers of any temporary majority be limited by long-term principles. To him it is not from a mere act of will of the momentary majority but from a wider agreement on common principles that a majority decision derives its authority (*Constitution*, p. 106).

Hence democracy, if it is not to harm liberty, must be based on a consensus across society about the limits of the majority's powers to coerce minorities.

These general postulates about democracy are followed by some extremely pessimistic views about the actual tendency of democracy since the late nineteenth century, above all its tendency to restrict and destroy liberty. The 'pernicious principle' of parliamentary sovereignty has allowed majorities in the legislature to accept no limits on their authority (*Law*, vol. III, p. 3), and has led to the erosion of liberty to the point of disappearance (*Constitution*, pp. 1–2; *Law*, vol. III, ch. 12; *Economic*).

Democracy, then, needs to be constrained by a constitution which limits the powers of government. This need for limitation is grounded on the actuality of modern democratic government, with its 'pork-barrel' character, its decline into a system of transient combinations of interests intent on using government for their own ends.

This constitutionalism is also linked to Hayek's epistemology, for the constitution will have to embody and enforce *traditional* values, against the claims of majorities to remake the world in the name of *reason*. Hence Hayek's veneration for the work of the archconservative Edmund Burke, who, unfortunately, despite his 'magnificent formulations' failed to provide a 'systematic theory' (*Law*, vol. I, p. 22).

What Burke did provide, above all, was a critique of the French Revolution as being founded on a greatly excessive presumption about the possibility of basing a reconstruction of society on reason, a presumption ignoring the centrality of custom and tradition, of facets of society not amenable to reason and social order (Burke, 1790/1968). Hayek identifies Burke with the British tradition in political philosophy, a philosophy, he argues, which from the eighteenth century diverged from the French tradition of rationalism. Unfortunately, the French tradition has been winning, and thus the West has tended fatally to ignore the fact that 'a successful free-society will always in a large measure be a tradition-bound society' (*Constitution*, p. 61). This is not an argument against the use of reason – indeed reason is a 'man's most precious possession' (*Constitution*, p. 69) but it is an argument against the arrogance of reason. His argument 'is an appeal to men to see that we must use our reason intelligently and that, in order to do so, we must preserve that indispensable matrix of the uncontrolled and non-rational which is the only environment wherein reason can grow and operate effectively' (*Constitution*, p. 69).

Human intervention in society's functioning should then be based on an analogy with the physician and the human body. Like a body, society is a self-maintaining whole which is kept going by forces we cannot replace. Change must be brought about by working with these forces rather than against them. Reform therefore should be piecemeal rather than wholesale (*Constitution*, p. 70).

Finally, Hayek's emphasis on the threat to liberty from the combination of democracy and rationalistic approaches to society leads him to specific but radical proposals for constitutional reform, which would involve a sharp separation of bodies concerned, on the one hand, with ordinary legislation, and, on the other, that concerned with the constitution, the body of rules of conduct binding on citizens and government alike (*Law*, vol. III, ch. 16).

Hayek is surely right to argue that the term *democracy*, like *liberty*, has been grossly overused, and that it has now got to the point where 'democratic' is used as a term of general approbation, with little precise content. Whilst there are clearly gains from the fact that today in Western Europe and North America almost all political forces feel required to call themselves democratic (Hirst, 1987), a restriction of the term's meaning would help clarify important issues. Thus those who do not at all share Hayek's political outlook can accept a definition of democracy on similar lines to his, as a means, as a mechanism, for choosing personnel for certain bodies (Hindess, 1983). However, this does not logically involve restricting the notion of democracy to public, political bodies, as Hayek alleges (*Constitution*, ch. 7). It makes perfect sense to talk of 'industrial democracy', for example, as long as it is clear the term refers to a *means*, election of personnel for decision-making bodies within enterprises. (The issue of industrial democracy is returned to in the final chapter.)

Hayek's argument against the unrestricted rights of majorities to impose any legislation on a minority is also well taken. The difficulty here is not the principle, but the actual nature of the limits on the power of the majority and the mechanisms for determining those limits.

On the nature of the limits, Hayek's appeal to a tradition of shared values which must underlie such constitutional limitations takes us rather little of the way to resolving difficulties if there is dispute about the existence of such a consensus, let alone the problem of how it is to be divined. It is obvious that constitutional limits on the capacities of legislatures are inherently political, in the sense that to a greater or lesser extent they embody different views about desirable forms of social organisation. Thus, for example, one can imagine a constitutional limit on the capacities of a legislature to restrict the rights of private property. There is plainly no consensus on such an issue in many Western countries.

On constitutional mechanisms, Hayek has committed himself to highly specific (and radical) proposals for a complete separation of powers between a legislative assembly, determining rules of conduct binding on the second house, and the parliament, which would make laws within the rules laid down by the legislature. The former body would be constituted by 'cohort elections', where every year all 45-year-olds elected some of their number for a 15-year period of service. The idea behind this striking proposal is that such persons would be well-established members of the community, chosen by their peers, who would be paid and pensioned sufficiently to be independent of any interest-group pressure. This assembly's task would be substantial and difficult. It would have to make rules explicitly, which in the past had been based on 'not yet articulated conceptions implicit in past decisions by which the Courts should be bound' (*Law*, vol. III, p. 109).

The peculiarity of Hayek's proposal for the mechanism of choosing membership of the legislative assembly plainly arises from the desire to secure a body independent of interest groups. But this must be to chase a chimera. Interest groups are ubiquitous in any society with long-lived institutions, and it may be that to try to avoid their influence is to attempt the impossible. It would be better to have *explicit* interest-group representation in a second chamber, thereby making the claims of those groups public and open to scrutiny (and challenge). Such a proposal could involve, for example, producer groups, consumer groups, different economic sectors (e.g. agriculture), regions, and ethnic groups.

As Paul Hirst (1986, pp. 121–2) has argued:

> One great advantage of a substantial corporatist component in a wider political system is that it forces us, in devising such representation, to ask what 'interests' matter, and why – in

particular to consider not only strongly organised interests and lobbies but also those interests that are poorly organised or unorganised. A formal system of corporatism has the advantage that it provides channels of influence for those without the informal power to lobby that stems from prestige or possession of resources (see also Hirst, 1989, pp. 71–6).

Such an approach stems from taking the claims of parliamentary democracy seriously. It recognises that in such democracies one can never abolish the powers and capacities of bodies other than parliament – parliament can *never* be effectively sovereign. So the need is to develop a range of other forms of democracy; not to replace parliament, but to subject government to scrutiny and accountability in a way which parliament by itself could never achieve.

But whatever the merits of turning Hayek's interest-group argument on its head, it does not deal with his major notion, that of grounding constitutional limits on the assumption that there exists a set of rules waiting to be articulated, and which will be largely (there is some provision in his scheme for appeals to a constitutional court) accepted without major dissent. Again, this does not seem to deal with the inherently political nature of any such rules.

Hayek's discussion of constitutionalism is, as noted above, based on a strong distinction between tradition and reason. Reason is a very limited instrument, to be used with a great deal of discretion, and with due regard to the traditions and customs of the society to be reformed.

Two points may be made on this issue at this stage.

First, the implications of stressing that the limits of our reason only allow for piecemeal reform is very unclear. Clearly, it would rule out a Kampuchean-style 'Year Zero' – societies cannot be remade as if writing on a blank sheet of paper without catastrophic consequences. But this limit case apart, what are the boundaries of acceptable reformism? As noted above, Hayek uses the analogy of the physician and the body in his argument. But what are the limits of medical intervention? We may all agree that broken bones may be set, but what about heart transplants or cell-replacement therapies? Outside the limit case, Hayek offers us little guidance. The concept of 'piecemeal reform' seems largely empty of meaning once we move from philosophical generalities to discuss any specific proposals for social reform.

Second, we may note the radicalism of Hayek's own reform proposals. There are the reforms of the constitution noted above, which would fill traditionalist defenders of the House of Lords (and many others) with horror. Even more radical are his proposals for the 'privatisation' of money (*Denationalisation*) as the only effective way of preventing inflation. These proposals are defended as being required by the dire state of the world. But that, of course, is how radicals always justify their proposals. How do these proposals escape the hubris, the 'fatal conceit', of other reformers' programmes?

Law

Hayek's emphasis on the importance of tradition is closely related to his conception of law. For him, law, properly defined, is not the promulgation of legislative bodies, but a body of rules which have evolved over a long period, but which may never have been articulated. Law does not give specific orders to individuals on how to act (that is done by commands), but provides an (always imperfect) degree of certainty within which they make their decisions in pursuit of their own ends (*Constitution*, pp. 150–1; *Law*, vol. I, chs 4, 5). Thus law has no purpose except that of providing order: 'Law is therefore not a means to any purpose, but merely a condition for the successful pursuit of most purposes' (*Law*, vol. I, p. 113).

Law in this sense is vital for the protection of that private domain (including private property) that alone allows liberty. 'Law, liberty and property are an inseparable trinity' (*Law*, vol. I, p. 107). Hayek does not ground his view of law on any idea of 'natural rights' (e.g. a natural right to own property) as was suggested by David Hume. But he argues that law, as it has evolved, has had a content which follows Hume's idea of such laws of nature. This content has three characteristics: 'stability of possession, of transference by consent, and of the performance of promises' (*Constitution*, p. 158).

Law, as a product of evolution and the embodiment of tradition, should not be radically remade in the name of excessive rationalism. This is what Hayek perceives that Bentham and the utilitarians of the early nineteenth century proposed – a remaking of law on rational principles (*Constitution*, pp. 174–5). Hayek rejects this and celebrates instead the British common-law tradition of a slow accretion and marginal emendation of rules, which permits the adaptation of law to changing circumstances, but in accordance with the broad thrust of the overall pattern of rules. Thus law-making is a rational process, a matter of maintaining the *consistency* of the law (*Law*, vol. II, p. 43). But law must not be subjected to the 'constructivist' rationalism which would start from a blank sheet of paper. Hence, wherever possible, the common law is to be preferred to statute law, which is inherently likely to be based on such rationalism.

If the essence of the law is a body of rules which originate not in a sovereign will or body, but in an evolutionary interaction between changing circumstance and human attempts to apply (limited) reason to building up those rules, then, Hayek argues, it is law, not people, that rules. The law does not allow particular groups to use the law to attain their ends, but provides a framework of means for everyone to pursue their own ends. Here, then, one can see the basis of the idea of the 'rule of law' which is so important to Hayek. This, like the invisible-hand concept in economics, allows the individuals' pursuit of their own ends to be compatible with an overall order, an order which has not been designed, but is a 'spontaneous order', a product of evolution.

For the rule of law to function there must be an underlying agreement on the values that rule embodies. Hence the idea of the rule of law is a 'meta-legal' doctrine or a political ideal. The idea must come to form part of the 'moral tradition' of the community (*Constitution*, pp. 205–6). This requires general agreement not on the ends of action but on what shall count as just conduct in the pursuit of differing ends (*Law*, vol. I, p. 95).

Hayek distinguishes private law, basically concerned with rules of conduct, from public law, concerned with the rules of organisation of government (*Law*, vol. I, p. 132). His prime concern is with the former, with what is mainly the common law, that is, law made by judges, not by statute. To provide the high degree of certainty required by the rule of law, the amount of discretion in legal decisions must be very limited. Judges must play the role of 'experts in law', interpreting the law but not using discretion in the sense of imposing their own will on decisions. 'The task of the judge is to discover the implications contained in the spirit of the whole system of valid rules of law or to express as a general rule, when necessary, what was not explicitly stated previously in a court of law or by the legislator' (*Constitution*, p. 212).

Broadly speaking, judges will be guided by the generality of expectations about what the law is, though there will be cases where expectations differ, and the judge will have to make a decision which most logically follows from the generality of rules, or which serves the same function as the generality of rules (*Law*, vol. I, pp. 115–16).

However, the development of common law may be imperfect, and require legislative intervention to correct its direction of development. The most common reason for such a reversal to be required is probably 'that the development of the law has lain in the hands of members of a particular class whose traditional views made them regard as just what could not meet the more general requirements of justice' (*Law*, vol. I, p. 89). Such class bias, Hayek argues, has affected major areas of English law, including the laws on the relations between master and servant (i.e. labour law), landlord and tenant, creditor and debtor, and organised business and its customers (*Law*, vol. I, p.89). However, these problems, while requiring legislative intervention, do not invalidate the general notion of the rule of law as a bulwark of freedom.

As already noted, Hayek's view of law is grounded in his evolutionary approach to human institutions. The law embodies the accumulated wisdom of past generations, which is a wisdom our limited human rationality can never fully encompass. One problem with this evolutionism is where one draws the line between 'proper' evolutionary development, and the wrong roads down which class bias and other factors may lead judges to take the law. One way of focusing this issue would be to ask how we are to treat the evolution of greater restrictions on the rights of private property over, say, the last 150 years in many Western countries. Is this part of the evolutionary process to be applauded, or one of those wrong tracks which needs legislative intervention?

Equally, if the judges across such a broad range of important issues went the 'wrong way' as Hayek alleges, and this requires reform 'of whole sections of the established system of case law' (*Law*, vol. I, p. 89) where does this leave the case against 'rationalistic' reform of the law? Hayek provides us with no jurisprudential principles which would provide a clear answer to such questions.

Judicial discretion clearly operates in Hayek's view of the world, however much that does not fit with his view of how the rule of law should function. But, Hayek argues, whilst the rule of law can never be fully realised, 'if it is represented as an impracticable and even undesirable ideal and people cease to strive for its realisation it will rapidly disappear. Such a society will quickly relapse into a state of arbitrary tyranny. This is what has been threatening during the last two or three generations throughout the Western world' (*Constitution*, pp. 207–8).

Certainly the rule of law is important; if it means freedom from arbitrary arrest and imprisonment, equality of treatment before the law, and a largely stable and predictable pattern of rules on which to base our behaviour, few would, presumably, argue with it as an ideal. But the concept of the rule of law means more than this.

It rests on the notion of the legitimacy of the political process which is outside, or prior to, the law-making process. The 'law' cannot, logically, determine the limits of law. Hence Hayek is obviously right that the idea of the rule of law is a *political* ideal and one with inherently conservative implications. It is not just a doctrine about legal due process, but it is also about how law is to be limited as to what it can do – it cannot go beyond the political limits which lie behind its existence. Of course, Hayek can justify these political limits by appealing to a consensus said to underlie the rule of law – but this is little more than a gesture, supported by no evidence.

Some democratic socialists have supported the notion of the rule of law. E.P. Thompson (1975, pp. 258–69) has rightly attacked the crude Marxist notions that law is simply a mask disguising the interests of the ruling class. Such a reductionist approach not only is inadequate as an historical account of law and its effects, but also implies that some day law can be abolished when class antagonisms have disappeared under communism. But such a picture of the future is untenable: it assumes that there will come a time when all conflicts of interest are abolished and social order can be preserved without law. More particularly, it assumes that big government will cease to need to be checked by (amongst other things) legal restraint – surely a *highly* dangerous presumption.

The trouble with the notion of the rule of law is that it is necessarily a fiction. This notion suggests that law somehow escapes from its unavoidable determination by specific agencies, and in so doing masks the fact that what we always have in fact are laws in the plural, not 'law', and that these laws can and do conflict. This homogenisation of law rests further on a notion of sovereignty; law is unified by its emanation from the presumed site of sovereign power; in modern states, from the legislative authority (Hirst, 1986, pp. 24–6).

All this means that the notion of the 'rule of law' is necessarily mystificatory. It obscures the sources of laws, and the extent to which these have to be related to specific institutions which create them. Law is homogenised into some vague essence before which we can only bow down in awe and wonder.

To be sceptical of the concept of the rule of law is emphatically *not* to endorse the view that we should look to a future where law is abolished, nor is it to celebrate the unbridled rule of discretionary agencies. Indeed, it is perfectly logical to be critical of the doctrine of the 'rule of law' and argue for the desirability of an extension of legal constraints on, most especially, big government (Hirst, 1985). The point is not to call for the extension of 'law' *per se*, but of particular *forms* of law, notably public or administrative law, as a complement to the common (judge-made) law which traditional defenders of the rule of law, like Hayek, have relied on. But, as recent commentators on the British constitution have noted, '"The common law" is one of these most effective of all pieces of mystification. Almost to the same extent as the rule of law itself, it has been invested in Britain with magical powers and its rhetoric has at times even echoed what Rousseau called the General Will' (Harden and Lewis, 1986, p. 37).

But whatever the historical role of the common law, it is plainly inadequate as a defence against the arrogant claims of big government based on the rhetoric of parliamentary sovereignty. What is needed is not, as Hayek suggests, the abolition of big government, but its more effective control by a framework of public law. But public law in this context would be not part of a seamless web of law but one institutionally specific way of regulating public power. And to be effective such public law would have to exist alongside other forms of regulation – including democratisation of government agencies, clear limits on the administrative capacities of state bodies, and much freer flows of information about the grounds for decision-making in government.

The notion of the rule of law 'came to encapsulate a

complex moral aspiration: the legitimacy of public power' (Harden and Lewis, 1986, p. 5). That aspiration remains a compelling one. The difficulty is, as Harden and Lewis argue, that much of the debate on the rule of law implies that the institutional framework within which that doctrine was first fully enunciated, nineteenth-century democracies with a very limited franchise, remains intact. But in the modern world of mass democracy and big government it acts as an obstacle to thinking through the practical implications of that aspiration.

Whilst many accept that the doctrine of the rule of law is an inherently conservative one, even nonconservatives may argue that to attack the doctrine is, as Hayek alleges, to threaten to bring the world tumbling about our ears. The argument is that once we see that the law is inherently discretionary – is rule by men (and a few women) not law – then this will mean a loss of faith in the impartiality of law which must bring anarchy in its wake. But this is a hard doctrine to justify. In its day-to-day workings we know the law is highly discretionary; in the criminal area we know the political process determines where police resources are deployed, what count as serious crimes to worry about and prosecute, and what crimes are pursued by prosecuting agencies. Prosecution decisions quite explicitly involve consideration of public policy, not just the question, 'Has a law been broken?' And this is to leave aside all the discretion which inhabits judges' decisions, discretionary here as much as in the areas covered by Hayek's account. Yet knowing this, I and many others continue to obey (most of) the law. Why should I be so arrogant as to suppose that I am any different in this regard from other citizens? Surely it may be argued that 'law' is brought more into disrepute if we pretend that it could be something it can never be, rather than accept that it is an inherently discretionary business and openly debate the appropriate procedures for determining and regulating the limits of that discretion.

Justice

For Hayek, justice can apply to human conduct. Justice is abiding by the rules of conduct laid down by law. These rules of conduct are abstract, i.e. they do not relate to any *specific* purpose, but only to the preservation of order in which individuals can pursue their own ends with a degree of certainty. These rules are the product of an evolutionary process, which has developed from a persistent effort to bring consistency into a system of rules inherited by each generation (*Law*, vol. II, pp. 31–3).

Clearly, justice is here equated with law properly so called – with private and criminal law which regulates the conduct of citizens. Justice and law in this sense mainly consist of prohibitions, and must be universal in application, i.e. apply both to every person (or class of persons) and to an unknown number of future instances.

> Since the consequences of applying rules of just conduct will always depend on factual circumstances which are not determined by these rules, we cannot measure the justice of the application of rule by the result it will produce in a particular case ... That it is possible for one through a single just transaction to gain much and for another through an equally just transaction to lose all, in no way disproves the justice of these transactions (*Law*, vol. II, p. 38).

Hayek's account of what he means by justice is obviously linked with his notion of law, as discussed in the previous section. It follows closely the traditions of conservative legal philosophy, particularly of David Hume (1738/1968, book III, part II). What is much more striking in Hayek's discussion is his application of this doctrine to modern concerns, above all his attack on the concept of social justice.

Part of Hayek's disdain for this expression is based on the looseness with which the adjective *social* is deployed. 'I see in the ambiguity of the word and the slovenly manner in which it is normally used a very real danger to any clear thinking, to any possibility of reasoned discussion with regard to a great number of our most serious problems' (*Studies*, p. 238; see also *Fatal*, pp. 114–6). But the term *social* not only involves lack of clarity and vagueness, but also brings unwelcome effects in its train:

> First, it tends pervertedly to insinuate a notion ... that what has been brought about by the impersonal and spontaneous processes of the extended order is actually the result of deliberate human creation. Second, following from this, it appeals to men to *re*design what they never could have designed at all. And third, it also has acquired the power to empty the norms it qualifies of their meaning (*Fatal*, p. 116).

What brings especial criticism by Hayek is the linking of the adjective *social* to the noun *justice*. Indeed he has written a whole book attacking this notion (*Law*, vol. II): 'I have come to feel strongly that the greatest service I can still render to my fellow men would be that I make the speakers and writers among them thoroughly ashamed ever again to employ the term social justice' (*Law*, vol. II, p. 97).

This hostility is grounded on two propositions – that in a market/spontaneous order the phrase has no meaning; that attempts in the name of such justice to impose a centrally determined distribution of incomes will destroy that market order and the freedoms it embodies (*Law*, vol. II, pp. 66–7). For Hayek, justice is about rules of conduct, not outcomes of conduct. It is about how people conduct themselves, not the pattern of outcomes which follows as unintended consequences from that conduct. Hence the income distribution which flows from a market order cannot be judged just or unjust – it is not the intended consequence of human action. Indeed Hayek goes out of his way to separate a market-determined distribution of incomes from any notion of merit attaching to the recipients of those incomes.

Hayek recognises that it is a convenient argument in favour of a market economy that it generates income relative to merit: 'It has been argued persuasively that people will tolerate major inequalities of the material positions only if they believe that the different individuals get on the whole what they deserve ...' (*Law*, vol. II, p. 73). But, for Hayek, this link is simply not true. The rewards individuals receive are related to the market's valuation, i.e. the value as perceived by consumers of the goods and services produced, and 'these values which services will have to their fellows will often have no relation to their individual merits or needs' (*Law*, vol. II, p. 72). Thus the justification for market-determined rewards cannot rest on a notion of 'just deserts' in the sense of a proportional relation between effort or merit and those deserts. Rather, that justification can come only from the incentive effects of rewarding those who provide what people want to buy: 'It is still in the general interest to proceed on the presumption that the past success of some people in picking winners makes it probable that they will also do so in the future, and that it is therefore worthwhile to induce them to continue their attempts' (*Law*, vol. II, p. 73).

Second, Hayek argues, the pursuit of justice in rewards must lead to governments attempting to determine the incomes of particular persons rather than defending rules by which people take their chances in the market order. This determination of incomes is objectionable on two grounds – it will undermine the workings of the market as an economic system, and it will lead to greater and greater interventions in personal domains, and hence, if pursued, to totalitarianism. The first objection we will return to in Chapter 4. But the second one is obviously the relevant one here, in the discussion of Hayek's general social and political philosophy.

Part of the problem with discussing the notion of 'social justice' is to decide how far the arguments are purely semantic. Hayek is surely right that both the adjective *social* and, in particular, its conjunction with *justice* have been bandied about with great looseness. It would undoubtedly be a gain if the terms were used with a great deal more discretion and accuracy. But acceptance of a plea for greater clarity in the use of language is not of course the same as accepting Hayek's pleas that the term 'social justice' be abandoned. Plainly, as Hayek obviously understands, advocates of social justice are almost always advocating reductions in material inequalities, inequalities of income and wealth. Hence the substantive issue is not whether we use 'justice' to judge income distributions, but whether we can make a case for greater equality, or whether, as Hayek alleges, attempts to bring this about will undermine not only the economy but also freedom and (real) justice.

Hayek is surely right to say that the claim that in a market system material rewards are linked to any criteria of merit is a myth. One issue which arises from this is whether a social order is sustainable where no such link is present. Conservative critics of Hayek have tended to argue that it is not (Kristol, 1971). One response to this position (though hardly congenial to conservatives) is to argue that the pursuit of a more egalitarian distribution of incomes will, at least in part, correct the perceived 'injustices' of a market system. Such an argument is, of course, a little ambiguous for egalitarians, for it suggests that the search for equality may actually mitigate hostility to a market system which constantly tends to generate inequalities.

But our concern here is not with the case for equality, but with whether its pursuit has the dire consequences suggested by Hayek. Again Hayek's argument depends very much on the idea of society as based on irreconcilable principles – either a principle of the market, in which rewards are wholly unrelated to merit, or an egalitarian system where individual rewards are decided by some all-encompassing merit table. Plainly this last *would* be an extraordinarily controversial, complex and intensive business. It would be akin to a universal Charity Organisation Society, seeking out the infinite gradations of the deserving.

But this nightmare is not relevant. It is perfectly possible for the state to intervene in the distribution of incomes via tax and benefit systems without this kind of invasion of private domains. Of course these mechanisms are 'rough and ready': they do not and cannot embody a wholly consistent criterion of merit. But such systems can be broadly designed to reduce inequalities without addressing questions of individual merit. It is the disparities in the overall income distribution which such systems can be aimed at correcting, not the place of particular individuals in that distribution. Of course, how far this process should go will be partly a question of trading off the claims of equality against the claims of economic incentives for efficiency – if, indeed, there is such a trade-off (see Chapter 5).

The market order and claims for 'social justice'/egalitarianism are not irreconcilable principles between which societies must choose, but co-existing forms of organisation in most Western states. That co-existence can never be non-conflictive nor unchanging. But it has not led and need not lead to a breakdown of the social order. Ultimately, the test of whether policies for reducing equality threaten freedom, as Hayek suggests, is an empirical one; we have had substantial periods of such policies in Western Europe, and we can try to gauge their effects on freedom (see Chapter 5 below).

3
Evolution, Reason and Morals

Hayek's work contains a metahistory which functions as a critique of what he sees as the intellectual foundations of socialism. The three key areas of this metahistory are his accounts of evolution, of reason and of morals.

Evolution

Central to Hayek's metahistory is his commitment to a strong concept of social evolution. He argues that Darwinian notions of biological evolution, of natural selection, have a very close analogy in societal development, in that forms of social organisation have been selected historically.[1] Evolution has selected societies with rules that are most conducive to human survival, this being demonstrated by the multiplication of human numbers they have allowed (*Fatal*, p. 20).

Like Darwinian evolution, social evolution for Hayek has no purpose and does not proceed through any predetermined stages (*Law*, vol. I, pp. 23–4). Rather, chance variations in social organisation were selected because they led to the prosperity of those groups which adapted them:

> That rules become increasingly better adjusted to generate order happened not because men better understood this function, but because those groups prospered who happened to change them in a way that rendered them increasingly adaptive. This evolution was not linear, but resulted from continued trial and error, constant 'experimen-

tation', in arenas wherein different orders contended. Of course there was no intention to experiment – yet the changes in rules thrown forth by historical accident, analogous to genetic mutations, had something of the same effect (*Fatal*, p. 20).

The mechanisms of this evolution differ from those of Darwinian biology. The 'decisive factor is not the selection of the physical and inheritable properties of the individuals but the selection by imitation of successful individuals and groups; what emerges is not an inheritable attribute of individuals but ideas and skills – in short, the whole cultural inheritance which is passed on by learning and imitation' (*Constitution*, p. 59).

Thus what Hayek offers is a history of cultural evolution in which we can observe the gradual and interrupted development of institutions and rules of conduct which facilitated the growth of what he calls an extended order, the crucial feature of this order being the suppression of the primitive instincts of solidarity, altruism and group decision. The development of the extended order required that these instincts be replaced by abstract (i.e. not end-related) rules of conduct – saving, widely distributed property ownership, honesty, etc. Large groups cannot develop the division of labour and raise their numbers on the basis of instincts; this requires the development of an order in which individuals can pursue their own ends within a framework of stable expectations about how others will behave. Those groups that stumbled on these abstract rules developed this extended order and were successful in evolutionary terms, i.e. they multiplied in numbers, whilst those that maintained instinctual characteristics eventually perished (*Studies*, ch. 4; *Fatal*, p. 70).

Hayek's story of evolution is a history of the rise of civilisation. For him civilisation is synonymous with the extended order, and, in turn, this extended order rests on private property and free markets. Hence in so far as Hayek attempts to flesh out his evolutionary schema with evidence, that evidence is basically concerned with the development of private property and markets since Graeco-Roman times (*Fatal*, chs 2, 3). Developments prior to this are explicitly excluded from any empirical support, on the grounds that practically no evidence exists (*Law*, vol. III, p. 156; *Fatal*, pp. 30–1).

For Hayek, the history of the growth of civilisation since antiquity is a history of episodic progress in the spread of private property and markets, interrupted only too frequently by the activities of governments. Where governments were strong, markets waned; where governments were weak, trade and civilisation advanced together. Thus 'nothing is more misleading, then, than the conventional formulae of historians who represent the achievement of a powerful state as the culmination of cultural evolution: it as often marked its end' (*Fatal*, p. 33).

This story of the episodic but clear progress of the extended order through most of human history is interrupted by two forces. The most important, for Hayek, is intellectual, the rise of what he calls constructivist rationalism from the eighteenth century. The other is sociological – the rise of a large category of persons whose daily life blinded them to the rules necessary for the success of the extended order.

The intellectual content of constructivist rationalism is returned to in the section below on reason. Here the issue is how this fits into Hayek's evolutionary schema. He argues that rationalists, beginning with the French philosophers Descartes and Rousseau, had combined that rationalism with an unworkable notion of freedom, which focused on freeing people from restraints. For Hayek, this represents a rejection of precisely what made civilisation possible – the suppression of instincts by the acceptance of the evolving rules of conduct of the extended order.

It was Rousseau who – declaring in the opening statement of *The Social Contract* that 'man was born free, and he is everywhere in chains' and wanting men to be free from all 'artificial' restraints – made what had been called the savage the virtual hero of progressive intellectuals, urged people to shake off the very restraints to which they owed their productivity and numbers, and produced a conception of liberty that became the greatest obstacle to its attainment (*Fatal*, p. 49).

Following Rousseau a whole series of other intellectuals have fallen prey to the same error. Because of this by the end of the nineteenth century serious discussion of the role of private property in the development of civilisation had more or less ceased (*Fatal*, p. 50). This litany of error persisted into the twentieth century, perverting the arguments of great thinkers like Keynes, Einstein, Bertrand Russell and Freud. Strongly influenced by these intellectual sources, governments have been led to actions which undermine private property and the market, and, in consequence, have undermined the basis of freedom.

The other source of diversion from the progressive evolution of the extended order was its basis in the growth of large-scale industry and commerce. Within such organisations people lose their contact with market forces, and grow to misunderstand and reject the logic of the market (*Law*, vol. II, p. 81; *Constitution*, pp. 121–3).

Hayek's story of evolution thus fits into his general pessimism about the trend of developments since the late nineteenth century, which he sees as a period of growing collectivism, undermining the gains previously obtained from the development of individualism (e.g. *Constitution*, pp. 1–2). But beyond merely 'fitting-in' with Hayek's other positions, evolution is clearly crucial to his whole approach. Why is it so central?

First, a concept of evolution, that is, of purposeless but incremental and progressive change, opens up a space for a crucial role for *tradition* in social life. This is returned to in the section on reason below. Second, such a concept of evolution enables Hayek to tell a story of the benign progress of capitalism (see also *Capitalism*). Whilst for Hayek the process of evolution has no purpose, he is clear that the evolutionary pattern is one of progress, of the development of civilisation to higher levels. He quotes Montesquieu to this effect: 'Où il y a du commerce, il y a des moeurs douces' (*Fatal*, p. 38).

The ultimate measure of that progress is human population size (*Fatal*, ch. 8). For Hayek, the expansion of population is a sign that capitalism has provided the necessary (but not sufficient) conditions for the expansion of civilisation.[2]

There are a number of problems that can be identified with Hayek's evolutionary story.

First, in any evolutionary schema there is the issue of what is selected for. In other words, which characteristics of social groups are the basis of their survival; which of their disappearance. Here one can only note that Hayek is extremely vague – for example, he suggests that religions which encourage strong families (undefined) provide favourable evolutionary conditions, but he never spells out this point in any detail (*Law*, vol. II, p. 87; *Fatal*, ch. 9). This is a large hole in the argument, because he suggests that certain characteristics are crucial to evolutionary progress, but does little to identify what these characteristics are (Barry, 1979, p. 82).

The second problem concerns the context and mechanisms of evolution. All accounts of social evolution tend to assume that throughout most of history people have been forced to respond to urgent problems of physical survival and adaptation to the environment; otherwise there is no pressure to cause evolutionary success or failure. But

> man has no significant non-human predators. Even hunters and gatherers have a significant degree of control over the production of necessities so that their life is far from being constantly threatened by want, scarcity and privation ... Human beliefs, institutions, and practices like art, kinship and religion consume a great deal of time and energy, but they are neither necessarily adaptive to the environment nor productive of social order (Hirst and Woolley, 1982, p. 89; see also Sahlins, 1974, ch. 1).

In other words, it is far from clear that human populations normally face the environmental pressures that force animal populations to 'adapt or die'.

For Hayek, the predominant mechanism of evolution is imitation – the successful are initiated in their social practices by the unsuccessful. Imitation seems both a weak mechanism for explaining social change and one difficult to reconcile with the historical record of displacement of one form of social organisation by another. On this latter point Hayek seems guilty of a moralistic form of argument common on the Right. Because capitalism is believed to be beneficent, then, in this argument, its origins and history must be benign. This may be contrasted with the classic Marxist approach where capitalism is seen as undoubtedly progressive, but its history as bloody and violent. This would seem more consonant with the historical record. One obvious example would be the USA where the displacement of Indian civilisations by capitalism rested predominantly on genocide rather than imitation.

Hayek is true to his ancestry of eighteenth-century thinkers like Montesquieu and Adam Smith in believing that capitalism's legitimising of self-interest will suppress the 'passions' of war-making and violence. Unfortunately, we now know this to be a fairy tale (Hirschman, 1977).

Another problem with the parallel drawn between biological and social evolution is that modern ideas of the former offer a clear analysis of what it is that is passed on from one generation to another – the gene. But what is the parallel mechanism in social evolution? Hayek never tells us very clearly how 'traditions' and 'rules of conduct' pass from one generation to another. The social analogy with the gene remains a mystery. (On notions of evolution as applied to the economy, see Hodgson, 1988, ch. 6.)

For Hayek, the selection procedures of social evolution are interrupted by the state – the state functions to inhibit the development of the extended order and civilisation. This raises two difficulties. On the one hand there is the question of the historical record. Hayek's account completely ignores what many see as the crucial role of the state in making possible the rise of capitalism (e.g. the classic work of Polanyi, 1944). More important, perhaps, is the idea that this whole evolutionary process has been stalled or reversed over the last 100 years or so because of the increased intervention of the state. For Hayek, the rise of 'collectivism' since the late nineteenth century is an interruption to the evolutionary process. At its most general level this idea of an interruption to evolutionary progress is not a problem for Hayek's argument – he perceives evolution as never having been smooth and continuous. However, the characterisation of this recent interruption would seem to raise a number of difficulties.

First there is the obvious problem that this alleged evolutionary regression has been accompanied by an unprecedented period of expansion of population (and economic growth), the expansion which Hayek uses as his central measure of evolutionary progress. He never attempts to deal with this striking contradiction.

Lying behind this evolutionary regression in Hayek's account are two factors: the primary one is intellectual error leading to misplaced government intervention; the second, less important factor is the rise of the large corporation, severing substantial portions of the population from contact with market forces and thereby engendering hostility to a market system. On the first aspect it may be noted that this invokes a quite different mechanism of evolution than elsewhere suggested. Evolution, instead of being a selection among institutions and the rules of conduct they embody, becomes a selection among theoretical ideas via their impact on the role of government. Hayek's argument also greatly exaggerates the role of theory in *initiating* the changing role of the state in the economy over the last century. (Though in the development of his work over time it is probably right, as Bosanquet [1983, p. 36], suggests, that Hayek has put less emphasis on collectivist ideas and more on democracy in explaining the increased role of the state.) This general point is discussed further in Chapter 4, but one example brings out the issue very clearly.

The example is the role of the state in the monetary system. Hayek in recent writings has argued the case for private issue of money to prevent governments from causing inflation by excessive money creation, supporting this with the view that the government's role has been one of unwanted interference driven by political considerations (*Denationalisation*). In this way the case for private money is supported by a story of evolutionary progress interrupted by 'external' intervention by the state. But this will not do. As Congdon (1981, p. 17) argues, the emergence of a monetary role for the state can be given a far more plausible, invisible-hand, evolutionary explanation:

> Contrary to Hayek's argument in *Denationalisation of Money*, private agents gradually and spontaneously, without artificial impetus from government, chose one bank as a lender of last resort; they accepted its note liabilities as means of payment; and the bank so chosen was banker to the government. It follows that the government could not have – and cannot now – escape responsibility. The provision of a sound currency is a necessary function of the state.

Hayek's other argument for the interruption of evolutionary progress in the last 100 years is essentially sociological. It links a shift in public perception to changes in economic organisation. As Barry (1979, pp. 142–3) notes, this argument is paradoxical for Hayek's general schema:

> Undoubtedly, the emergence of the large-scale enterprise is part of the spontaneous evolution of the market order yet it would appear to be accompanied by a set of values which are not merely inimical to the market order but are agents of its destruction. It would seem to be the case that as the market evolves it creates a moral order antithetical to its further evolution in a spontaneous manner.

This paradox would seem to be part of a wider problem in Hayek's writing, of specifying the institutions and values which support his extended order. As noted above, he makes very general references to the importance of the institutions of the family and religion, but on values there is an equally large problem. A constant theme of Hayek's work is that collectivism and modern socialism represent an atavism, a re-emergence of 'primitive' values which cultural evolution has failed to suppress. This atavism is seen as gaining its force from the survival of old instincts amongst the masses, combined with the intellectual power of constructivist rationalism which Hayek sees as proposing a form of liberty which in fact represents a licensing of those instincts. In the modern period, supporters of this error have, according to Hayek, included both Keynes and Freud.

It has to be said that when he is discussing Keynes and Freud, Hayek's standards of argument tend to deteriorate fast. For example, as noted in Chapter 1, Hayek's discussion of Keynes's phrase 'in the long-run we are all dead' involves a grave distortion of the meaning of that remark. Equally distorting is his view that Keynes's social philosophy encouraged the revival of 'atavistic' emotions and passions. Indeed, as Hirschman (1977, p. 134) points out, Keynes shared Hayek's view that the rise of the legitimate pursuit of self-interest under capitalism would suppress previous forms of undesirable social behaviour, and Hirschman quotes Keynes's famous argument, 'It is better that a man should tyrannise over his bank balance than over his fellow citizens' (Keynes, 1936/1973, p. 374).

Hayek, like his fellow countryman Karl Popper, is plainly outraged by Freud – and is just as crude in his attacks on Freud's work. (On Popper see Williams, 1975; Popper dedicated his famous book *Conjectures and Refutations* to Hayek). Hayek's view that Freud is amongst those who in the twentieth century have encouraged a crass libertarianism, a form of liberty which suggests an unconstrained expression of human instincts, is just plain wrong. He asserts that Freud's 'basic aim' was 'undoing the culturally acquired repressions and freeing the natural drives' (*Law*, vol. III, p. 14; see also *Fatal*, pp. 18, 153). In fact Freud argued that all societies necessarily repress and direct the basic drives towards certain ends. The purpose of psychoanalysis is not to free the drives from restraint but successfully to channel them in certain directions which would not produce neurotic symptoms (Freud, 1930, p. 104; Hirst and Woolley, 1982, pp. 140–3).

Hayek's treatment of Freud is symptomatic of the cavalier approach that Hayek's evolutionary schema leads him into. His evolutionary account is indeed a 'fabulous tale' (Belsey, 1986, p. 180). It is replete with contradictions, embodying, for example, a notion similar to the orthodox Marxist concept of primitive communism, whilst Hayek declares elsewhere (*Law*, vol. I, p. 108) that this concept is a myth which 'has been completely refuted by anthropological research'. Its account of the mechanisms of evolution is vague in the extreme, and the history used to support the case is cursory and tendentious. We can agree with conservative critics of Hayek that it is unhelpful to see history 'as a single evolutionary process' without accepting the implication drawn by such critics that *any* notion of human progress is to be discounted (Gray, 1988, pp. 257–8).

Reason

Much more interesting and serious is Hayek's discussion of reason. This is in part related to his account of evolution, because he sees evolution as having 'gone wrong', largely as a result of the excessive role played by the claims of reason in human affairs since the eighteenth century.

Hayek divines two traditions of thought, what he calls critical and constructivist rationalism. The first of these grew out of the Scottish Enlightenment, notably in the works of David Hume, Adam Smith and Adam Ferguson, followed by writers like Edmund Burke. The second derived its inspiration from Descartes and is represented by Rousseau, Condorcet and the Physiocrats. The first of these lines of thought was empirical and unsystematic, and based itself on the interpretation of traditions and institutions which had spontaneously grown up and were imperfectly understood.

The second was speculative and rationalistic, aiming at the construction of a utopia (*Constitution*, p. 54; *Law*, vol. I, ch. 1).

The critical rationalists used their reason in the context of institutions which have evolved, and which embody the wisdom of a slow process of accretion of tradition. This tradition embodied far more knowledge than reason could encompass:

> Civilisation was the accumulated hard-earned result of trial and error; that it was the sum of experience, in part handed from generation to generation as explicit knowledge, but to a larger extent embodied in tools and institutions which had proved themselves superior – institutions whose significance we might discover by analysis but which will also serve men's ends without men's understanding them ... (*Constitution*, p. 60).

In this schema, primitive human instincts were held in check by institutions which had grown up in the manner outlined in the discussion of evolution above. Thus the tradition was linked to the idea of human fallibility and sinfulness, and only the force of circumstance would make people behave economically and adjust means to ends. In this framework, reasons is not all-powerful, but has to be used intelligently, within the 'matrix of the uncontrolled and non-rational which is the only environment wherein reason can grow and operate effectively' (*Constitution*, p. 69).

The alternative to this tradition, as Hayek sees it, is that of constructivist rationalism, which allows no limits to the scope of reason. This approach refuses to accept the usefulness of anything that cannot be ascribed to reason. It believes that society can and should be constructed on the basis of rational principles: 'Morals, religion and law, language and writing, money and the market, were thought of as having been deliberately constructed by somebody, or at least as owing whatever perfection they possess to such design' (*Law*, vol. I, p. 10).

Hayek is willing to call reason 'man's greatest possession' (*Constitution*, p. 69), but he believes that the use of reason must recognise the *limits* of reason. Civilisation has progressed more by *unintended* adaptation to circumstance than by application of reason. This approach to the limited role of reason is summarised in the following passage:

> It is simply not true that our actions owe their effectiveness solely or chiefly to knowledge which we can state in words and which can therefore constitute the explicit premises of a syllogism. Many of the institutions of society which are indispensable conditions for the successful pursuit of our conscious aims are in fact the result of customs, habits or practices which have been neither invented nor are observed with any such purpose in view. We live in a society in which we can successfully orientate ourselves, and in which our actions have a good chance of achieving their aims, not only because our fellows are governed by known aims or known connections between means and ends, but because they are also confined by rules whose purpose or origin we often do not know and of whose very existence we are often not aware (*Law,* vol. I, p. 11).

This construction of two totally distinct lines of thought in political philosophy is typical of Hayek's desire to see the world divided into the good and the bad. It is very doubtful whether in fact this dichotomy is sustainable. For example, as Barry (1979, pp. 63–4) points out, utilitarianism fits uneasily into the 'constructivist rationalist' category. Also, as Barry again points out, Hayek attempts to dismiss laissez-faire as an excessively rationalist doctrine. Hayek believes that this argument tries to work from an abstract principle rather than from the evolved traditions of society. In this example Hayek would seem to be placing a weight on tradition which leaves little room for *any* role for reason – most laissez-faire writing has been grounded on a 'pragmatic' account of human action rather than on 'abstract principle'.

This question of the weight given to tradition would seem

to be the crux of the issue of Hayek's discussion of reason. On the one hand Hayek is a Burkean conservative, for whom the weight given to tradition is such that almost every existing social arrangement is sanctified as the product of evolutionary development which could be changed only at great peril. On the other hand, he is sufficiently a rationalist to advocate radical reforms to the constitution and the monetary system (chs 2 and 4). This must leave the reader puzzled as to what actually are the limits of reason proposed by Hayek.

We can unconditionally accept Hayek's arguments that to talk about society as if it were a blank sheet of paper on which anything may be written is both analytically unacceptable and likely to lead to catastrophic consequences if acted upon. But this kind of Pol Pot politics seems totally remote from anything on the agenda of politics in the advanced institutional countries in the twentieth century. In particular, no variety of democratic socialism, which Hayek sees as his main intellectual enemy, proposes reforms which would be ruled out by such a basic argument. Of course, such reforms would be ruled out by Burkean conservatism, but that would seem to be difficult to make compatible with *any* use of reason, so it would be difficult to make compatible with the idea of reason as 'man's greatest gift'.

So Hayek's discussion of reason would seem to offer no unambiguous criteria of 'acceptable' and 'unacceptable' deployments of reason within the political programmes currently on offer in the advanced capitalist countries of Western Europe, North America, Japan or Australasia. As a current example from the politics of these countries, we have the issue of privatisation of natural monopolies like water and electricity. Are these privatisation moves 'rationalist constructivism', being based on *a priori* reasoning about the benefits of market competition, and against the grain of traditions of public-utility provision; or, alternatively, acceptably rational as an extension of the already existing predominance of market forms of provision? Hayek's criteria would seem to offer no help on such an issue.

A further problem of Hayek's discussion of reason is the assumption that doctrines of 'constructivist rationalism' have been crucial in the development of socialism and communism. Hayek endorses Talmon's (1952) argument that in this philosophical regard there is a direct line of descent from Rousseau to the Russian Revolution. The Gulag Archipelago is immanent in *The Social Contract*. Not only is this implausible as history, but it ignores the strong evolutionist tendency in Marxism, which in its own way asserts the importance of historical antecedents for social change, 'the new society maturing in the womb of the old', as Marx famously put it in the Communist Manifesto.

Indeed, intellectually the most rationalistic arguments in recent years have not been from the socialist Left but from the neoclassical Right.[3] Such arguments raise profound problems (e.g. Hindess, 1988). But, these problems noted, there remains a problem in conceiving of how arguments about forms of social organisation (i.e. political arguments) can be conducted which are not substantially 'rationalistic' in character, i.e. assume that politics proceeds on the basis of rational argument. Political arguments have to be framed in terms of rational principles, even if we know at the same time that human action can never be reduced to rationality in motion. But only the most unthinking conservative can resolve this dilemma by appeal to what *is*, rather than through any rational justification for forms of social organisation. In other words, political activity is unavoidably predicated on an overly rationalistic view of how societies function. But such rationalism is by no means a step on a road which must lead us to Year Zero.

Finally, the limits of Hayek's appeal to custom and tradition must be noted. He rightly treats social organisation as depending very much on implicit rules, on customs and traditions which are taken for granted rather than articulated. The implicit assumption he makes is that all those customs and traditions are benign. But, of course, it is a key point made by, among others, modern feminists that they are not benign; it is precisely such unspoken assumptions that are central to women's subordination. So part of a feminist politics must be to make these customs and traditions explicit in order to challenge them and their effects. A similar point can be made about emerging forms of green politics.

Morals

Perhaps Hayek's most frequently quoted sentence is David Hume's 'the rules of morality are not the conclusions of our reason' (Hume, 1738/1968, vol. II, p. 235). Rather, morality is the evolutionary product of generations of interaction between human beings and their environment, which has produced a tradition of rules of conduct which underlie much of everyday life.

> To understand our civilisation, one must appreciate that the extended order resulted not from human design or intention but spontaneously; it arises from unintentionally conforming to certain traditional and largely *moral* practices, many of which men tend to dislike, whose significance they usually fail to understand, whose validity they cannot prove, and which have nonetheless fairly rapidly spread by means of an evolutionary selection – the comparative increase of population and wealth – of those groups that happen to follow them (*Fatal*, p. 6).

Not only have rules emerged simultaneously with, and made possible, the extended order of the market. What is to count as moral conduct and the justice which embodies rules about that conduct has to be linked to that extended order. In 'primitive society' what Hayek calls 'instinctual' conduct, such as solidarity, co-operativeness and altruism, was appropriate, but such tendencies require to be severely circumscribed in market society. Instead a market society requires that rules of conduct support private ownership of property, sanctity of contracts, competition, individual gain, privacy, legitimacy of trade and exchange (*Fatal*, p. 12).

Thus Hayek's notion of morality is a relativist one, in the

sense that his preferred order of morality is compatible only with an extended market order. But he would also claim that the scale of population made possible by that extended order, and therefore that morality, would be incompatible with socialist morality, which therefore 'endangers the standard of living and the life itself of a large proportion of our existing population' (*Fatal*, p. 9). Socialism does this by encouraging moral rules which disrupt and destroy the market order. It encourages an overextended altruism and notions of co-operation and neighbourliness which are threats to the types of *abstract* rules which large-scale extended societies require. Socialism appeals to the atavistic instincts rather than to the painfully evolved tradition of morality properly speaking. 'I believe that an atavistic longing after the life of the noble savage is the main source of the collectivist tradition' (*Fatal*, p. 19).

This broad-brush dichotomy is qualified by the acceptance that in 'sub-orders' these old instincts have their place: 'Solidarity and altruism continue to retain some importance by assisting voluntary collaboration, even though they are incapable, by themselves, of creating a basis for the more extended order' (*Fatal*, p. 18). So people must learn to live in two sorts of world at once. But Hayek's main concern is to resist the extension of rules of conduct appropriate to a 'micro-cosmos', e.g. a family or voluntary association, to the extended, market order. The most inappropriate extension of rules of morality from one sphere to the other is in the area of income and wealth distribution. For Hayek, these distributions are not the object of moral criteria because they are not the consequence of deliberate human choice.

> There is no need morally to justify specific distributions [of income or wealth] which have not been brought about deliberately but are the outcome of a game that is played because it improves the chances of all. In such a game nobody 'treats' people differently and it is entirely consistent with respecting all people equally that the outcome of the game for different people is very different (*Law*, vol. II, p. 117).

Hayek's discussion of morals is largely concerned with what may be called the moral conditions of economic life. Only secondarily is he concerned with issues that figure in a broader concern with moral conduct in a broader sense,[4] though on occasion he links constructivism to the erosion of moral standards, in the sense of notions of right and wrong, and to the erosion of the idea that there are objective rules of just conduct (*New*, pp. 15–18). The erosion of standards is also linked to the erosion of a sense of individual responsibility. This, in turn, is linked to the development of the welfare state, with its alleged tendency to increase dependency upon state provision (*Constitution*, ch. 5).

Hayek's argument that the rules of conduct which we normally obey are often implicit and conventional, rather than formalised and the obvious product of a reasoned argument, seems incontrovertible. What is much less clear is what the implications of this argument are.

First, to accept the implicit and 'unreasoned' character of many rules of conduct is not to accept the description of such rules as evolutionary in any strict sense of that word. Evolutionary implies a process which both embodies progress and which is nondeliberative. Neither of these seems to be the case in the development of morals. To characterise morals as progressing involves accepting Hayek's implicit teleology of moving towards an extended order which is superior to previous forms of social organisation. As noted in the first section of this chapter, such a notion of evolutionary progress is deeply problematic.

Second, to accept the idea of the development of morals as largely nondeliberative is unacceptably to 'naturalise' the process of moral change. In the case of Britain, for example, we can see much of the eighteenth and nineteenth centuries as a period of 'moralising the poor' against deeply ingrained moral attitudes (e.g. Thompson, 1963). Deeply ingrained but not instinctual; Hayek's account of a triumph of (limited) reason over 'instinct' is an account which serves only to denigrate previous 'primitive' norms of conduct, largely as a polemical device to accuse socialism of pandering to an atavistic desire to return to such instincts.

Also, as Barry (1979, p. 82) points out, the evolutionary approach to morals is necessarily retrospective – it can argue that such-and-such rules have survived and infer from this some evolutionary benefit from that survival. But it cannot identify those rules which are crucial for the survival of a society at the time, so even in its own terms the approach is of rather little use in knowing what rules to create and enforce *now*.

Hayek's views on the scope of moral obligations are plainly of great importance for democratic socialists, who have traditionally seen co-operation, solidarity, fraternity and general altruism as crucial components of the principles they stand for. How seriously need socialists take Hayek's argument that the effective scope of our moral obligations is limited, and that we should not attempt to 'moralise' the unintended consequences of action such as the distribution of income? Hayek is surely quite right that if we overextend our perception of our moral responsibilities, everyday life becomes unworkable. For example, it makes no sense to try to form a moral judgement of the consequences of writing this book, in the sense of trying to decide whether it is acceptable for me to deprive another author of income on books which may fail to be sold in competition with this.

Clearly if any role for the market is accepted (see Chapter 5) this must involve acceptance of some scope for competition, and hence for leaving the financial consequences for producers of decisions taken by consumers to be determined in the marketplace. I cannot sensibly make hundreds of moral decisions about the consequence of my purchases for producers every time I visit the supermarket. (Though it is perfectly reasonable to make specific moral judgements in this context – for example, not to purchase South African goods.) But does that suggest that I give up any sense of moral responsibility which goes beyond my immediate neighbours and associates, as Hayek implies? In particular, does it make all moral judgements on the broad distribution of income and wealth absurd and potentially dangerous, as Hayek alleges?

Conservative commentators on Hayek have pointed to the dangers of his argument that the distribution of income in market economies is not an issue of morality, because such an argument undermines a basic case for capitalism, i.e. that there is some relation between effort and reward (Gray, 1984, pp. 50–1). Hayek is on strong ground when he asserts that it is very difficult to see that capitalism does proportionately reward effort or merit in any other sense, rather than often rewarding good fortune (*Law*, vol. II, ch. 9). Hayek accepts that this poses a dilemma for defenders of capitalism – how far are they to encourage the belief in the rewarding of merit, knowing this not to be how capitalism works? (*Law*, vol. III, p. 74). Hayek's solution on occasions seems to be to appeal to uncritical rule-following, bolstered by religious beliefs on the necessity of social order (Gray, 1984, p. 57). This would seem to be an abdication of the 'critical reason' he espouses elsewhere.

This dilemma cannot be evaded by democratic socialists who believe in any role for the market – they too will have to ask how they are to deal with the inescapable absence of any direct relation between effort and the reward generated by the functioning of markets. Unintentionally Hayek supports half the traditional socialist case against large inequalities of income; by stressing the lack of a link between effort and reward he undermines any moral case for such inequalities. The case for inequality is therefore a purely pragmatic one, and solely depends on empirical estimates of the nature and extent of any benefits from such inequality for the growth of income, resulting from inequality's effects on incentives to producers.

Hayek's suggestion that the socialist ideals of solidarity, altruism and co-operation are likely to threaten the whole life of the population seems almost actively perverse in the context of advanced capitalist countries today. We may concede to his arguments that a social system which assumed each individual had responsibility equally for the welfare of every one of the millions of others in a society would be nonsense. But this is surely not the problem. What we see in the advanced capitalist countries is not a dangerous overextension of solidarity and altruism. On the contrary the picture is much more one of invasion of the 'microcosmos' by the capitalist values of the market order.

We also need to note that the extended, market order is much less a sphere of pure competition than Hayek suggests. Relations between many of the core units of competitive capitalism, i.e. enterprises, have been and are, perhaps, increasingly characterised by co-operative *as well as* competitive behaviour (Hirst and Zeitlin, 1989). So a social ethic of competition is much more problematic for supporters of capitalism than Hayek suggests.

Hayek's basic dilemma in the field of morals is to combine a very limited sense of what type of situations we can pass moral judgements upon with a strong sense of the need for a sense of individual responsibility in society. This latter he sees (though an agnostic) as being bolstered by religious belief (*Fatal*, ch. 9). But whilst it may be accepted that historically, if less obviously today, religion did have certain positive features for maintaining norms of conduct, we also need to note the severe restrictions such beliefs imposed on conduct and the anxieties so caused. In any event, this is surely one area where we can be fairly sure there is no going back – in the West, at least, secularisation is here to stay.

Equally one may accept Hayek's argument that some notion of individual responsibility and related categories is essential for civilised existence (*Constitution*, ch. 5). Most modern socialists would accept that such categories

> do not depend on individuals being in some inherent, ontological sense responsible or guilty, but they do require that conduct is attributable to individuals, not as its origin but as its locus. They may be held responsible for their acts, except in certain specified cases of incapacity, without us believing those acts arise from purely consciously determined purpose (Hirst and Woolley, 1982, p. 132).

The problem with Hayek's argument is that he ties his notion of individual responsibility to a common theme of the Right attack on the welfare state – that the effect of state-provided welfare has been to erode individual responsibility and encourage dependency. Such a view has been nicely demolished by Goodin (1985). He points out that there is clear empirical evidence that state welfare does *not* encourage 'dependency'; that, in practice, ending state welfare brings not 'individual responsibility' but dependence on families, which is far more arbitrary than state welfare, and that the whole notion of welfare dependency assumes an implausible view of character formation.

In sum, Hayek's claim that complex modern societies require a framework of 'morals' or norms of conduct to survive cannot be doubted. Equally, that to secure such a framework is a problem in modern Western societies may also be accepted by those who share few of his other views. But to postulate that the threat to such a framework comes from an unholy alliance of socialist doctrine and popular atavism is to enter a world of make-believe which can find no support from a serious study of what socialists are saying, nor from an honest account of where the pressures on previous norms of conduct come from.

Concepts of evolutionary progress seem particularly unhelpful in this area. As contemporary socialists have written,

> No civilisation can provide its members with means of conducting themselves that depend entirely for compliance and performance on utilities, pleasures, satisfactions and reasons. Means to resolve conflicts, cope with failures and suffering, endure everyday dullness are necessary in every social order ... Our problem is that for all our wealth, technique, and knowledge, indeed, in part *because* of them, we lack the ideational means to order and justify social actions often possessed by many 'poorer' and more 'ignorant' peoples (Hirst and Woolley, 1982, p. 138).

Liberalism or Conservatism?

A useful way of summarising Hayek's arguments in the areas of evolution, reasons and morals is to discuss the undoubted tensions in his work between his liberalism and his conservatism.

As noted in Chapter 2, Hayek sees his project as being to restate and rebuild the case for liberalism. And his emphasis on liberty as the key political value obviously places him in the liberal camp. On the other hand, his social theory has strongly conservative aspects. The veneration of tradition, the emphasis on the evolutionary origins of morals, the limits to the capacity of reason all fit a conservative cast of mind.

In the postscript to *The Constitution* Hayek concluded his work with a piece entitled 'Why I am Not a Conservative'. There he argued that for all his reverence for long-lived institutions, a reverence shared by conservatives, he believed that the necessity then was for radical change. The trouble with conservatism is that, lacking its own distinctive view of the future, it is content to act only as a brake on change rather than to try to give that change a distinctive direction. Hayek believed that, lacking a coherent social theory, conservatives would too readily rely on an obscurantist appeal to authority, which would make possible in some circumstances an excessive denial of liberty by coercing what a liberal would regard as the private sphere. Finally, Hayek emphasises that liberalism has faith in the development of new knowledge. 'Though the liberal certainly does not regard all change as progress, he does regard the advance of knowledge as one of the chief aims of human effort and expects from it the gradual solution of such problems and difficulties as we can hope to solve' (*Constitution*, p. 404).

Hayek's combination of liberal and conservative themes is fundamentally related to his philosophical position. On the one hand he draws from Kant the desire to establish universal principles of justice, which would imply having a rational, legitimising foundation for the social order. On the other hand, from David Hume he draws the arguments on the limits of human reason, the centrality of tradition, and hence the dangers of 'constructivist rationalism' and any desire to reconstruct society on the basis of rational principles. Another way of putting this is to say that Hayek's attempt to make liberalism a universal doctrine is inherently a rationalist enterprise, bound to be in conflict with the scepticism of a Humean emphasis on human ignorance.

As Kukathas (1989) has argued, Hayek never satisfactorily solves this central dilemma of his thought; Hume and Kant can form only an 'unstable alliance' (Kukathas, 1989, p. viii) as the basis for his arguments.[5] This is linked to Hayek's central ambiguity, mentioned several times in this book. What are the limits of reason, and hence which projects for social improvement can be accepted as stemming from the proper use of reason; which must be dismissed as dangerously rationalist? Here Hayek goes no further than Hume, stressing the need for caution in the rational reconstruction of society, but providing no clear guideline to the limits to such reconstruction (Kukathas, 1989, p. 18). This ambivalence permeates all of Hayek's work, and undercuts most of his attempts to ground discussion of economic and social policy as an overarching philosophical scheme.

Notes

1. Hayek argues that Darwin adopted his theories from pre-existing theories of social evolution, e.g. *Constitution*, p. 59. Compare Hirst and Woolley (1982, p. 6).
2. Using population size as a measure of progress is of course extremely problematic if the forms of economic activity which sustain that population are themselves unsustainable, because of their effects on the ecological viability of the planet. This issue cannot be addressed here, where I have focused on assessing Hayek's argument in its own terms.
3. But some Marxists have attempted to refound the Marxist tradition on a rational action basis (e.g. Elster, 1985).
4. This area is less than straightforward in Hayek's writings. At one point he stresses the historical role of religions in revolt

against property and the family (*Fatal*, p. 57), but at the same time he argues that monotheistic religions especially have been important in developing and preserving the customs and traditions necessary for the extended order (*Fatal*, p. 135).
5. It has been persuasively argued by Robbins (1961) that Hayek exaggerates Hume's conservatism, which is too readily linked to the work of Burke. See also Harrod (1946).

4

Full Employment, Inflation, Welfare and Trade Unions

Whilst the bulk of Hayek's work has been concentrated on broad issues of economic, social and political philosophy, he has always been willing to draw conclusions for current events from this theoretical work. This leap is especially apparent in *The Constitution*, the last third of which consists of a wide-ranging critique of much of what we may call the post-war consensus, the combination of full-employment policies, the acceptance of a degree of inflation, the commitment to state welfare provision and the acceptance or encouragement of strong trade unions which characterised most of the advanced capitalist world from 1945 to the mid-1970s.

Hayek has lived long enough to have been a critic of the thinking behind that consensus in the 1930s, before it came to be widely accepted, and to have been both a contributor to and a celebrant of the demise of the consensus in the 1970s. His criticisms had been little heeded during the post-war boom of the 1950s and 1960s, but the onset of the crisis of the early 1970s created an opportunity which he seized. He had intervened little in economic policy debates for some years. 'By the summer of 1974, however, the problem of inflation had become so alarming that I felt it to be my duty once again to speak out' (*New Studies*, p. 192). In that decade Hayek actively engaged in polemics on policy, and emerged as a major guru of those conservative political forces, especially in Britain and the USA, opposed to the post-war consensus.

The purpose of this chapter is to outline and criticise Hayek's arguments on the major strands of policy involved in the post-war consensus. The broader philosophical positions discussed in the previous two chapters are largely taken as read, and the focus here is, by contrast, on the manner in which Hayek analysed both the reasons for and consequences of public policy-making after 1945.

Full Employment and Inflation

For Hayek one of the worst features of the post-war period was its persistent inflation. Inflation, he argued, causes 'grave harms', the chief of which is that it gives 'the whole structure of the economy a distorted, lop-sided character which sooner or later makes a more extensive unemployment inevitable than that which that policy was intended to prevent' (*New Studies*, p. 192). This argument parallels that produced by Hayek in his analysis of the depression of the 1930s, notably in *Prices* (see Chapter 1, above), where the inflationary boom of the 1920s was seen to have distorted the economy, these distortions eventually having to be put right in the following period of unavoidable unemployment. The length of the post-war boom generated particularly large distortions, and hence much higher unemployment would inevitably result once the inflation ceased (*New Studies*, pp. 193–5, 209–18).

Hayek traces the cause of the inflation back to the work of Keynes and the Keynesians: 'The responsibility for current world-wide inflation, I am sorry to say, rests wholly and squarely with the economists, or at least with that great majority of my fellow economists who have embraced the teaching of Lord Keynes' (*New Studies*, p. 192). Keynes's error went back to a mistaken diagnosis of unemployment in the 1920s and 1930s. He was right that British problems in the 1920s resulted from an overvaluation of the pound at the time of the return to gold in 1925, but, Hayek argues, this overvaluation was being overcome by deflation until the forced and highly unfortunate departure from the gold standard in 1931. British unemployment in the 1920s was an almost unique episode in Hayek's eyes, because it involved a *general* excessive wage level (or inadequate level of prices). Unemployment, he argues, is nearly always *not* related to such economy-wide levels of wages or demand, as Keynes contended, but to inappropriate relative wages, which prevent the necessary movement of workers from contracting to expanding sectors of employment. Thus Keynes's analysis of an idiosyncratic episode in economic history was illegitimately generalised as a general theory of how economies may malfunction.

Keynes's emphasis on inadequate aggregate demand as the cause of unemployment led to expansionary budgetary and monetary policies in many Western countries in the post-war period in the attempt to maintain employment. The precise mechanism of that inflation was excessive expansion of the money supply, and in that sense Hayek's analysis follows that of monetarists like Friedman, in seeing a direct link from changes in the quantity of money to changes in the price level. But, for Hayek, the main damage wrought by inflation is not its effects on the *general* price level, as Friedman and other monetarists argue, but its effects on relative prices and hence the composition of output.[1]

For Hayek, Keynes's errors stemmed in part from the fact that he was 'a man of great intellect but limited knowledge of economic theory' (*New Studies*, p. 218). But they also stemmed from his methodological error, his belief in 'scientistic' explanations which focused on measurable variables. His theory, whilst appearing 'at first more scientific than the older micro-theory, it seems to me that it has achieved this pseudo-exactness at the price of disregarding the relationships which really govern the economic system' (*New Studies*, p. 289).

Keynes's analysis, Hayek suggests, was congenial to politicians because votes are always to be had for policies of cheap credit. Traditionally, politicians had been prevented from pursuing excessive credit creation by institutions like the balanced-budget rule (sometimes called 'the fiscal constitution'), the gold standard, fixed exchange rates and restricted international liquidity. Unfortunately, under Keynes's influence, the gold standard was replaced by the Bretton Woods system, whereby in 'its endeavour to place the burden of international adjustment exclusively on the surplus countries, i.e. to require them to expand but not to require the deficit countries to contract, [this system] laid the foundation of a world inflation' (*New Studies*, p. 201). Even worse was to follow when, in the early 1970s, floating exchange rates replaced fixed rates for most currencies, which 'constitute the practically irreplaceable curb which we need to *compel* the politicians and the monetary authorities responsible to politicians to maintain a stable currency' (*New Studies*, p. 202).

Equally, Keynes's emphasis on aggregate-demand management undermined the previous rules that kept government spending low and enforced balanced budgets, i.e. the covering of all government expenditure by taxation, and instead allowed monetary creation flowing from fiscal deficits. In sum, Keynesian analysis offered politicians 'release from the most restricting fetters which had impeded them in their striving for popularity' (*New Studies*, p. 201).

By the 1970s, after an unexpectedly long delay, this process culminated in the acceleration of inflation which triggered Hayek's re-entry into policy polemics. At that point he argued that only three courses of action were possible. Either there would be a rapidly accelerating open inflation leading to complete disorganisation of the afflicted economies, or prices and wages controls leading inevitably to totalitarianism, or a sharp reduction in the quantity of money, halting the inflation in its tracks (*New Studies*, p. 197). The result of this last course, Hayek said, would inevitably be significant unemployment, but this would really be not the result of the restrictive policy but the inevitable consequence of the previous inflation.

The means to that monetary restraint that Hayek favoured was competition among currencies. He argued against Friedman's view that there should be a constitutional rule limiting the rate of growth of the money supply to some low percentage equal to the growth in the economy's productive potential. For Hayek, this approach relied on an unsustainable distinction between money and nonmoney, a distinction which does not exist in a developed credit economy (*New Studies*, pp. 207–8). He believed the gold standard would be an ideal framework for checking excessive monetary growth, but that this was unattainable. Hence he settled on 'denationalisation' of money as the solution. By removing governments' monopoly of legal tender, people would be able to choose among currencies and would choose those which maintained their value. Good money would drive out bad. This would discipline governments to limit inflationary monetary issues and put a stop to inflation (*New Studies*, pp. 218–31; *Denationalisation*).

Like many writers on the Right, Hayek emphasises the dangers of inflation. However, the emphasis within his case against inflation is an idiosyncratic one. Most discussion of the harms of inflation sees it as damaging the workings of a market economy by causing confusion over the information given by relative price changes to producers and consumers. Such changes in relative prices get confused with the absolute price changes which characterise inflation (Friedman, 1977). This process undermines the efficiency of the market economy because producers and consumers are not responding to the appropriate signals as to the real costs and prices of goods, generating lower levels of output and employment than under stable prices. By contrast, Hayek emphasises the impact of inflation on *relative* prices, which leads to the distorting of the structure of production until the inflation ends, when the distortions will have to be corrected by substantial unemployment.

In his discussions in the 1930s Hayek emphasised the distortions of inflation varying in different 'stages' of production – that inflation, above all, led to excessive investment in the capital-goods sector. However, the postwar inflation has been so long extended, he argues, that the way these distortions affect production has become totally obscured. The distortions are 'now spread much more widely, and the distribution is much more difficult to describe. It is a field I would wish some statistically minded economist would investigate in order to show how the process operated in particular countries. I am by no means sure where such an investigation would find the most important over-developments' (*New Studies*, pp. 212–13).

Although I am not questioning Hayek's good faith, this argument clearly provides a marvellous escape clause. One would have thought that if the chief harm caused by inflation was this distortion of production, a writer who put so much weight on defeating inflation would be able to provide *some* evidence for his thesis. As he makes clear in the quotation given above, he believes the evidence, in principle, is available, so to provide it would not seemingly be against Hayek's methodological precepts. Yet at this crucial point Hayek is reduced to wishing for others to produce the evidence.

Hayek does attempt to adduce evidence in support of his thesis when he tries to counter the argument that some countries have endured significant inflation for decades without this leading to disaster; for example, countries in South America. This argument is dismissed by Hayek on the grounds that these countries are 'predominantly agrarian', and thus do not suffer the distortions of industrial structure he perceives as the most damaging effect of inflation (*New Studies*, p. 203). 'Predominantly agrarian' is, however, an odd description of major inflationary countries in South America like Argentina, Brazil and Chile where in each case under 10 per cent of the population is involved in agriculture (UN, 1987).

Like many authors on the Right, especially writing in the mid-1970s, Hayek seems to lose all sense of proportion when discussing inflation. He notes how his view was affected by the fact that in his first job his salary rose 200 times in eight months (*New Studies*, p. 203), but this kind of hyperinflation bears little relation to even high-inflation countries in the developed world like Britain or Italy in the 1970s, where inflation peaked at around 20–25 per cent per annum. It is also a little hard to take seriously the argument that 'the present inflation has been deliberately brought about by governments on the advice of economists. The British Labour Party planned it that way as early as 1957', when the evidence cited for this claim is Labour Party estimates of inflation for 1960–80 used in discussion of policy for pensions (*New Studies*, p. 216).

This is not to argue that inflation 'doesn't matter'. For example, the 1970s inflation brought about significant arbitrary redistributions of income, notably by the negative real interest rates on building-society deposits. (Foster, 1976, provides evidence of this for Britain.) Recent careful research suggests that inflation even at relatively low levels may reduce investment by making the capital market work less effectively (Wadhwani, 1986 and 1987). But Hayek provides no good reason for any panic over inflation at the levels recently experienced in North America or Western Europe, nor for belief in his particular account of the effects of inflation. If there were serious danger of hyperinflation in the developed world, then his discussion would be important – but this has never appeared a serious possibility in any country in that category since at least the 1940s.

In explaining the reasons for inflation, Hayek gives an account of the post-war period which has much in common with those of many others on the Right, notably the public choice or 'economics-of-politics' school (e.g. Buchanan et al., 1978a). The starting point for this approach is that we should look at politicians in the same way that orthodox neoclassical economics looks at economic agents – as aiming to maximise their own ends (in this case votes), subject to constraints (Downs, 1957). This leads to analyses which see politicians not as ideologues but as agents providing voters with whatever packages of policies they want, under institutional constraints.[2]

This approach, notoriously, yields very different, even contradictory, conclusions, depending on the view taken about how voters calculate costs and benefits. For example, Downs (1960) argues that in democracies too little money will be spent on defence because voters see the costs, the taxes to pay for it, as more apparent than the more intangible benefits of deterrence which defence spending provides. Like most economics-of-politics accounts, this one could easily be reversed by making equally plausible, but equally unverifiable, alternative assumptions about voters' perceptions of costs and benefits. Thus it could be argued that the benefits of defence spending are substantial and obvious, whilst its costs, spread over the whole tax-paying public, are relatively small. The basic problem with these approaches is that they assume there is a 'correct' perception of costs and benefits which voters fail to achieve, but these correct perceptions are inherently arbitrary and act to allow their users to smuggle in political assumptions that they find congenial.

The economics-of-politics account of the post-war period, which Hayek adopts, sees the inflation of that period as being based on Keynes's undermining of the 'fiscal constitution' which constrained governments to low and balanced budgets. In this account Keynes legitimised public-sector deficits, unleashing the growth of public expenditure, budget deficits, and ultimately, in the 1970s, rampant inflation (Buchanan et al., 1978b; Buchanan and Wagner, 1977).

This account has a number of highly dubious features. First, the importance it gives to the writings of economists, even to economists as influential as Keynes, is surely overstated. In fact, the account adopts the Keynesian view of the importance of economic ideas, summed up in the famous words of Keynes (1936/1973, p. 383): 'the ideas of economists and political philosophers ... are more powerful than is commonly understood. Indeed the world is ruled by little else. Practical men who believe themselves to be quite exempt from any intellectual influences, are usually the slaves of some defunct economist'. Whilst Keynesians of course see the impact of Keynesian ideas on policy as beneficial, the economics-of-politics approach, followed by Hayek, accepts the same view of the power of Keynes's ideas, but treats the effects as disastrous.

This view of the importance of Keynesian economics to post-war policy is surely exaggerated. The commitment to full employment, which is usually seen as crucial in the post-war consensus, owed more to the impact of the Second World War than to any economic doctrine (Tomlinson, 1987; Booth, 1989). And such a commitment, explicit or implicit, was made in a range of advanced capitalist countries where Keynes was little known, but where the political effects of the war, especially in shifting the balance of power to the Left, were clearly felt.

Second, the actual path of development of the post-war period bears little relation to the economics-of-politics account. For example, Burton (in Buchanan et al., 1978a, p. 57) asserts that 'the effect of the Keynesian revolution was to remove the linchpin of the British fiscal constitution ... there was nothing to stop the drift towards the growth of expenditure and the running up of budget deficits in the British political system'. In fact, in Britain in the 1950s and 1960s, clearly a period following the Keynesian revolution, there was no tendency for budget deficits to increase, and the picture was one of budget current-account surpluses, with some borrowing to finance public investment in excess of these surpluses. The Public Sector Borrowing Requirement (PSBR: government expenditure minus government revenue) fell from an average of 7.5 per cent of government expenditure in 1952–9 (i.e. excluding the Korean War years) to 6.6 per cent in 1960–9 (Tomlinson, 1981, pp. 388–90). In other major countries there is equally no evidence of an upward trend in deficits in the public sector (Maynard and van Ryckeghem, 1976, p. 119).

Of course in the 1970s the level of public borrowing in most countries did expand sharply; in the British case, to peak at around 20 per cent of public expenditure in the mid-1970s. But the crucial point is that this sudden expansion was not the culmination of a long-term trend but an episodic event, a crisis. Indeed much of the economics-of-politics literature gained credence only from this crisis in the 1970s, which gave a superficial plausibility to its accounts.

Further, what caused the eventual reversal of the rise in the PSBR in the 1970s was not the constitutional checks that Hayek and the economics-of-politics school alleged were necessary, but the actions of financial markets, which refused to finance the deficits and forced a reversal of policy. Thus it is quite untrue that Keynesianism had led the way to an unconstrained expansion of fiscal deficits.

The economics-of-politics school shares not only the Keynesians' exaggerated assessment of Keynes's importance to economic policy, but also the Keynesians' exaggerated view of the importance of economic policy to the behaviour of the economy. As Matthews (1968) pointed out long ago, it is difficult to ascribe post-war full employment, even in Britain, the home of Keynesian economics, to Keynesian policies, when fiscal policy was usually slightly deflationary in the 1950s and 1960s. Rather, he suggests, we should see that full employment as primarily the result of the buoyancy of private investment and the expansion of international trade.[3]

Equally, the path of inflation is not easily related to Hayek's and the economics-of-politics school's accounts. Obviously, the trend level of inflation in the advanced capitalist countries was higher post-war than previously, but changes in the rate of inflation seem to be much better explained by fluctuations in commodity prices than by the direct effects of government policies. Thus the peak periods of inflation in North America and Western Europe since 1945 have been in the Korean War years, when commodity prices shot up owing to stockpiling; during the commodity and particularly the oil price rise of the early 1970s; and following the second oil-price hike in 1979 (Brown, 1985, ch. 1). So whilst the 1970s inflation was exceptional, it would be incorrect to see it as the continuation of an upward trend which continuously accelerated over the post-war years.

Hayek's account of the post-war international economic regime follows a line similar to his account of the internal regime. Here again Keynesian economists undermined the constraint on economic policy-makers by licensing a relaxation of the pressure on countries with balance-of-payments deficits in order to effect a deflation to correct the deficit.

> A great many of the most intelligent economists of our time, including most of my personal friends, have contributed to the destruction of the gold standard and the regime of fixed rates of exchange. They instituted something like the Bretton Woods system in which the whole responsibility for adjusting international balances was placed on the creditor countries, and the debtor countries were released of all responsibility (*New Studies*, p. 214).

This is a bizarre account of the Bretton Woods system and its consequences. It is true that the agreement did embody a 'scarce currency clause', whereby deficit countries could discriminate in trade against surplus countries if those surpluses were very large. But this, a response to the deflationary actions of countries like France and the USA between the wars in piling up trade surpluses and hence forcing deflation and unemployment elsewhere in the system, was rarely invoked. The idea that under the Bretton Woods system deficit countries came under no pressure to deflate is just wrong. Devaluation of currencies was allowed only under conditions of 'fundamental disequilibrium' and, as the British case of the mid-1960s well illustrates, countries rigorously deflated in order to maintain exchange rates in the face of payments deficits.

Finally, in this section we can look at Hayek's discussion of policies for reducing inflation. He is violently opposed to incomes policies, i.e. a direct role of governments in wage-setting, seeing them as a step on the road to a totalitarian economy. In this context there is a striking point about Hayek's range of references when discussing recent economic policy. Broadly speaking, only four countries figure in his account – West Germany and Switzerland as the virtuous, Britain as the plainly unvirtuous, and the USA always seeming likely to slip into sin. There is practically no reference to Scandinavian or, strikingly, Austrian experience.

These last named cases are precisely the countries where incomes policies have been successfully deployed over a long period to hold inflation rates down, with relatively little unemployment – and without slipping into totalitarianism (Therborn, 1986; Cameron, 1984). They are also and connectedly the countries whose 'corporatism' – bargaining among state, employers and unions – has brought the wage flexibility economists see as so desirable in the labour market (Bean et al., 1986).

It is of course true that the British experiment with incomes policy in the 1970s is not usually judged successful. However, most judgements can be significantly qualified. On the one hand, judgement of the general effects of such policies needs to consider their success in other countries in this period. Secondly, assessments of the British case are overly coloured by the dramatic breakdown of the policy in the 'winter of discontent' in 1978–9. A case can be made for the success of the earlier phases of the policy, certainly in comparison with what came after: 'From 1975–77 the incomes policy was a TUC triumph. It reduced wage inflation by 20 percentage points (from 28 to 8) with no further increase in unemployment, whereas Margaret Thatcher, faced with a similar crisis, rejected incomes policy and used an extra 2 million unemployed to achieve a small reduction in inflation' (Layard and Nickell, 1987, p.14).

The more general point is that incomes policies can be successful, but such success requires institutional conditions which are not easily achieved. For example, they require strong 'peak associations' of labour and capital, and a sufficient degree of political consensus to legitimise such deals as may be achieved by the social partners. These conditions were present in countries like Austria and Sweden but largely absent in Britain, and this was the problem of incomes policy, not its inherent economic defects or tendency to produce totalitarianism.

The record of Hayek's short-sharp-shock alternative to incomes policy is not encouraging. Whatever might be said about the British Conservative government's policies from

1979, they did bring a severe monetary deflation which failed to produce the change in expectations Hayek and others who supported such policies supposed. Indeed one of the most striking features of Britain in the 1980s has been the extent to which wage-setting behaviour has *not* been permanently changed by the very severe depression of 1979–82 (Cross, 1988).

As for more permanent institutional arrangements against inflation, Hayek has his own highly idiosyncratic proposal to end the existing monopoly issue of legal tender, and allow transactions in any currency accepted by the transactors (*Denationalisation*). This proposal for private money is seen as the logical economist's way to prevent the abuse of the government's monopoly powers, which have led not only to inflation but also to economic instability and unemployment. Hayek argues that a competitive regime of money issue would force note issuers to maintain the stability of their currency or lose customers to those who did. Gresham's Law would be reversed, and good money would drive out bad. Governments would be deprived of any instrument of monetary policy, and thus of the capacity to mismanage the economy.

In advocating this scheme, Hayek concedes the 'convenience' of a single-money system (*Denationalisation*, pp. 22, 55–6) but argues that the inconvenience of competing monies would be offset by the anti-inflationary benefits. Both sides of this equation may be challenged. As already noted, Hayek's emphasis on preventing inflation (as opposed to hyperinflation) is hard to justify given the limited evidence on its harmful effects. But even monetarist writers who accept the importance of defeating inflation find Hayek's proposals for private money hard to take seriously. Congdon, an orthodox monetarist (1981, p. 6) sums up the arguments like this:

> Our conclusion must be that Hayek's suggestions on the issue of a private Swiss ducat are unworkable. He talks confidently about replacing existing national currencies, without saying

why someone in his right mind should hand over valuable products in exchange for bits of paper. Unless these bits of paper can be converted into legal tender or another widely acceptable medium of exchange, there is no assurance they are worth anything. A bank certainly could issue index-linked note liabilities, with a guarantee of redemption into legal tender, but they are unlikely to become money. Since any price index can be calculated only from time to time, prices cannot be expressed in terms of indexed notes. They would therefore be inappropriate for normal payment functions.

The assumption from the classical economists onwards that a state monopoly of money issue is right and appropriate for the functioning of a market economy seems unshaken by Hayek's proposal.

Welfare

Hayek is profoundly hostile to much of the post-war development of the welfare state. He is happy to accept state provision of public amenities, e.g. parks;[4] of some minimum income security via both social insurance and 'charity'; and of provision of goods where there are substantial 'externalities' involved, i.e. where relying on the market will underprovide, as consumption levels will reflect only individual benefits and not the benefits which accrue to all from generally high standards of education or the prevention of infectious diseases.

For Hayek, what is undesirable in the welfare state is that its objectives go far beyond minimum income and service provision to embrace social justice and egalitarianism, and that in the pursuit of those ends coercion is used by the state, which claims exclusive rights to provide certain functions, and treats individuals unequally.

> The reason why many of the new welfare activities of government are a threat to freedom, then, is that, though they are presented as mere service activities, they really constitute an

exercise of the coercive powers of government and rest on its claiming exclusive rights in certain fields (*Constitution*, p. 258).

Hayek starts from the case for provision for the indigent. The old communities which used to provide support for the aged, sick and unemployed have broken down in modern, urbanised societies, he argues. Public provision is now necessary, 'be it only in the interest of those who require protection against acts of desperation on the part of the needy' (*Constitution*, p. 285). In wealthy societies such relief is likely to be at levels above a bare minimum, which will attract those who could otherwise have supported themselves. This justifies a compulsory insurance system, so that this latter category of persons will be forced to contribute to their upkeep. For Hayek, therefore, compulsory insurance *per se* is unobjectionable, unlike compulsory membership of a unitary organisation controlled by the state. The latter is objected to not only because it restricts evolution in the forms of organisation of insurance, but more importantly because it allows the use of the insurance principle to open the way to redistribution via the system of income maintenance: 'An apparatus originally meant to relieve poverty is generally being turned into a tool of egalitarian redistribution' (*Constitution*, p. 289).

The best system of income maintenance would be clearly two-tier. There would be a proper insurance scheme, whereby contributions generated unconditional rights to benefit when insured contingencies arose. Alongside this would be provision for indigence, with support only on the basis of proven need. Opposition to the latter, to the idea of the means test, is, he argues, 'wholly irrational'.

Two of the most dangerous parts of the welfare state are its provision for old age and for health care. In the case of old age, Hayek sees the provision of pensions to all, paid for out of current tax revenues (and hence from the income of those currently working) as inevitably leading to exaggerated claims for pension levels. This abandonment of the insurance principle in providing benefits is bound to lead to the pensions issue being a 'play ball for vote-catching demagogues' (*Constitution*, p. 296), who will buy the votes of the old with excessive pensions. This, in turn, will provoke such a response from the young who pay for the pensions that 'concentration camps for the aged unable to maintain themselves are likely to be the fate of an old generation whose income is entirely dependent on coercing the young' (*Constitution*, p. 297).

As far as health care is concerned, Hayek's particular target for attack is the British National Health Service (NHS). This is highly objectionable because, he argues, it is based on the notion that there is an objective standard of health care that could and should be met, and that such a system will pay for itself because of its impact on restoring the health of workers. The actual result of the NHS, he argues, will be infinite demand because of the zero price of care. This will lead to a misdirection of resources away from the temporarily incapacitated worker towards the chronic sick and aged. As a result, the NHS will lead to a bad average standard of health care for all. In addition, with doctors as the paid servants of the state, the way will be open to the political abuse of medicine, as in the Soviet Union (*Constitution*, pp. 298–300).

Hayek's discussion of the welfare state has, obviously, to be seen in the context of his broader attack on the notion of social justice (see Chapter 2 above). The key argument against the welfare state is that in pursuing the mirage of social justice it will diminish and eventually extinguish freedom. 'It seems to be the fate of all unitary, politically directed schemes for the provision of such services to be turned rapidly into instruments for determining the relative incomes of the great majority and thus for controlling economic activity generally' (*Constitution*, p. 303).

Because he concedes the case for the support of the indigent, Hayek has to suggest that there is a clear and significant dividing line between systems solely used for that purpose and those avowedly redistributive. But this line is a difficult one to draw because, as he admits (*Constitution*, p. 303), 'even the provision of a uniform minimum for all those who cannot provide for themselves involves some redistribution of income'. In fact, contrary to Hayek's specific assertions, the Beveridge inspired insurance system in Britain has never been a great engine of redistribution of income. This was because of its emphasis on flat-rate (rather than graduated) contributions and flat-rate benefits (Cutler et al., 1986, ch. 1). (Graduated contributions, with a ceiling, were introduced on a general basis only in 1975; some benefits were also graduated, but this has largely ceased in the 1980s.) The redistributive effects of such a flat-rate scheme are inherently limited.

Even taking into account the contribution of income tax to financing income support within the notionally 'insurance' system, and adding in the noncontributory part of the system (now called income support), the scale of redistribution by this part of the British welfare state is unremarkable. In 1985 those in the bottom 20 per cent of the income distribution table received 5.6 per cent of all income after taking into account tax and cash benefits (Hills, 1988, p. 9). More significantly, within the terms of Hayek's argument, that limited degree of redistribution has *not* been the primary purpose of the system. Rather, that purpose has remained the relief of poverty, however problematic that concept may be. Equally, the redistributive aspect of the system has *not* led to general state determination of income levels, which remain largely market determined.

Hayek's case for a two-tier system of income support seems equally ill-founded. On the one hand, the original Beveridge idea of 'insurance for all and for everything' which Hayek broadly endorses (though not as a single system) has been found to be incapable of satisfactorily coping with, for example, changes in the composition of households and the rise of the one-parent family. Hayek suggests that a nonunitary insurance system would be more flexible, but it is difficult indeed to see how such categories of person could be aided within any kind of truly insurance scheme. Perhaps, for Hayek, such persons should be relieved under the means-tested part of the system, to which all objections are 'wholly irrational'. Plainly, Hayek is not worried by the stigmatising aspect of means-testing – provisions under this heading are pure charity and issues of justice are particularly inappropriate (*Constitution*, p. 303, and footnote no. 37 on that page).

Hayek notes, only to dismiss, the important historical point that much of the opposition to means-testing from designers (not clients) of income-support systems arose from hostility to state discretion in determining income levels – an argument which might be thought to appeal to Hayek's brand of liberalism. Beyond this is the point that means-tested systems have been found ineffective in their own terms, because of the poor take-up rate of means-tested benefits. In Britain, for example, 25 per cent nonclaiming levels are common (Wilson and Wilson, 1982, p. 86). Equally, they are inefficient, in the sense that administrative costs are invariably much higher than insurance systems because of the detailed assessment procedures involved. Wilson and Wilson (1982, pp. 85–6) suggest that administrative costs are three times as high for means-tested benefits as for those provided by insurance.

If Hayek's discussion of the structure of income support seems ill-founded, his account of its consequences seems alarmist. Indeed, how little these alleged consequences have arisen is nicely illustrated when he moves from very general assertions as to future trends to more precise predictions. The idea that unconditional and universal pensions would generate a luxurious pension level until this created a revolt of the tax-paying young bears little relation to the history of pensions since the war. In a period when the voting influence of the old has increased with the ageing of the population, the pension in Britain has done no better than keep up with average earnings. In addition, the ratio of pensions to earnings cannot be considered high. National insurance pensions for a married couple have always been less than 50 per cent of the average wage, and even if supplementary support is added it has barely exceeded that level (Wilson and Wilson, 1982, pp. 53–7, 102–7). Not surprisingly, the revolt of the taxpayer against the subsidised luxury of the old has failed to materialise.

Like many on the Right, Hayek has particular hostility to the National Health Service part of the welfare state. In part this seems to derive from a belief that the NHS was based on a grand design for egalitarianism and social justice. As this illusion seems well established, even on other parts of the political spectrum (e.g. Le Grand 1982), it is worth emphasising that the NHS was based on no such single or simple objective. Rather, its aims were compounded of efficiency and rationalisation objectives on the part of politicians and bureaucrats; of the desire for access to the latest technology on the part of doctors; of the desire for equality on the part of socialists; and of minimum national standards by almost all those who supported its establishment. As Hindess (1987, p. 93; see also Klein, 1983, ch. 1) emphasises, 'the most important thing to notice is that egalitarian considerations played a very limited role in establishing the N.H.S. and in determining its organisational structure.'

Given this initial misunderstanding of the basis for the NHS, it is not surprising that much of the rest of Hayek's discussion is wide of the mark. He is right to note that the founders of the NHS were overoptimistic about the extent to which it would eradicate ill health, not appreciating that this is inherently a socially conditioned notion, and that demand for health care is likely to expand as higher incomes lead to higher expectations about health states. But the idea that demand for health care will be infinite because it involves no price is clearly erroneous. There is still an opportunity cost for many (especially working-class patients) in attending doctors' surgeries and hospitals, which is one reason why health spending in Britain is so unequally distributed (Le Grand, 1983, ch. 3). Equally, Hayek's prediction that the NHS would lead to 'excessive' expenditure on the old and chronically sick at the expense of the temporarily sick worker seems almost the opposite of what has occurred. Increasingly, since the 1970s, the DHSS has sought to guide resources away from excessive concentration in areas of acute medicine towards the old, the chronically sick, and the mentally ill and handicapped (DHSS, 1976; Command Paper 7615, 1979). Hayek's alarmism on this score has been controverted by the politics of resource allocation within the NHS, which has allowed consultants' preferences for high-tech medicine to put most resources into acute surgery and the like.

Hayek is also strongly opposed to the 'monopoly' aspect of the NHS. Of course, the NHS has not excluded private medicine, but certainly, at least until recently, this has not stopped the NHS very much dominating health care provision in the UK Such a domination has costs and benefits, though the costs, e.g. in terms of limited innovation and flexibility, will tend to be higher in a highly centralised system. The benefits, which Hayek completely ignores, have been efficiency, in the sense of delivering health care at low cost (Barr, 1988). Part of this low cost has been because of the near monopsonistic position of the NHS in the purchase of drugs and doctors' services. This has allowed some holding down of the inflation of costs of drugs, and doctors' salaries. The latter is particularly important, because medicine is inherently an area where the supplier of the service, the doctor, also has a major say in demand, given the lack of information held by the patient. Without some check on the doctor's capacity to generate demand for health care, such a situation is likely to lead to spiralling medical intervention and spiralling doctors' salaries with little impact on health, as is so strikingly the case in the USA (Barr et al., 1988).

Finally, it is worth stressing that Hayek's suggestion that the NHS would lead to the political direction of doctors was little more than scare-mongering. It totally ignored the strength of professionalism amongst doctors, which is not a simple function of their employment status.

The point being made here is not that the NHS is a marvel, the ultimate model of health care. It has, like any medical system, serious problems in the face of rising demand and costs. A fair summary of its achievements is given by Klein (1983, p. 177): 'If the aim of the N.H.S. is defined to be to eradicate disease and disability, then it is self-evidently a failure; if, however, its role is defined as being to minimise human suffering, then it can be reckoned a reasonable success story.'

This kind of conclusion can be generalised for much of the welfare state. It has failed to achieve the grandiose ends *some* of its designers hoped. Its consequences have sometimes been unforeseen and ambiguous. Plainly, it has had its problems as well as its successes, even before the assault on its principles in countries like Britain and in a more limited sense (because its existence was more limited) in the USA.

Nevertheless what seems clear in relation to Hayek's position is that most of his critique is crude. His arguments are simplistic, especially in assuming that the welfare state either did have or could have a single principle ('social justice') determining its development. Many of his critical points seem clearly *ad hoc*, and his predictions on the welfare state's development almost entirely wrong. Above all, his claim that its development would take us down the road to totalitarianism was unsubstantiated at the time by serious argument, and unsubstantiated subsequently by the way it has, in fact, developed.

Trade Unions

Like much of his discussion of the welfare state, Hayek's account of trade unionism focuses on the British experience, partly because he regards this example as a warning to other countries of what might follow if they go down the anti-liberal road. Whilst institutional details obviously differ, the principles offered in his analysis of the British case plainly have more general implications.

Whilst the increasing role of trade unions in Britain is a major part of what he believes has gone wrong in the post-1945, welfare-state period, the roots of this 'problem' are seen by Hayek as having an earlier and specific origin. This is the 1906 Trade Disputes Act. Under this act trade unions were granted general immunities in tort for actions relevant to industrial relations, whilst trade union organisers of strikes were granted protection from liability in a range of torts, notably conspiring and inducing breaches of employment contracts. These immunities protected union officials from claims for damages as long as they acted 'in contemplation or furtherance of a trade dispute', a term which became known as the 'golden formula' of British industrial relations law.

For Hayek the 1906 act was 'the most fateful law in Britain's modern history' (*Law,* vol. III, p. 31). By this act unions became 'uniquely privileged institutions to which the general rules of law do not apply' (*Constitution,* p. 267). These privileges are at the root of most modern British evils.

> These legalised powers of the unions have become the biggest obstacle to raising the living standards of the working class as a whole. They are the chief cause of the unnecessarily big differences between the best and worst-paid workers. They are the prime source of unemployment. They are the main reason for the decline of the British economy in general (*Unemployment,* p. 52).

So far has this shift in the legal status of unions gone that 'In general the legalisation of unions has come to mean that whatever methods they regard as indispensable for their purposes are also to be treated as legal' (*Constitution,* p. 274).

Under this legal framework, unions are so pernicious because they deny freedom in order to create monopolies, and then use those monopolies in ways which harm the general economic wellbeing. The key removal of freedom commonly achieved by the unions is their denial of the choice of individuals over whether to join a union or not. The crucial point is then the coercion of other workers: 'Most people probably still believe that a "labour dispute" normally means a disagreement about remuneration and the conditions of employment, while as often as not its sole cause is an attempt on the part of the unions to force unwilling workers to join' (*Constitution*, p. 268).

This assertion logically leads to the view that unions are effective in wage-bargaining only in so far as they obtain a monopoly control of labour supply, and thus raise the wages of the unionised at the expense of the nonunionised. Unions thus distort the market for labour: 'There can be no doubt that they cannot in the long-run increase real wages for all wishing to work above the level that would establish itself in a free market' (*Constitution*, p. 270). The effect is greater uniformity and rigidity of wages within union-controlled groups, and greater differentials between such groups.

Unions tend to limit the growth of real incomes both by keeping people out of high-wage industries, and by deterring investment, because they gain most power where investment is heaviest. Also their restrictive practices have reduced the efficiency of the investment which has taken place. But unions have broader damaging effects. First, they pressure governments into inflationary policies. Whilst inflation is caused by excessive monetary growth, not trade unions,

> Politically the problem of trade union power is the primary problem because, so long as government has the control of the supply of money, it will be forced to resort to the palliative of inflation which temporarily disguises the effects of a rise in wages on employment but leads to accumulated areas of omitted adaptations which merely stores up later trouble (*Unemployment*, p. 19).

Second, unions cause unemployment. They do this because they prevent the adjustment of *relative* wages which is the key to the labour market's adjusting to shifts in demand for products (*Unemployment*, pp. 55–6).

By the late 1970s Hayek's attacks on trade unions were becoming increasingly shrill. Unions had so denied the ideal of freedom of association that 'such freedom no longer exists for most workers. The present unions offer to a skilled worker only the choice between joining and starving ...' The reform of trade-union privileges was 'the price of salvation in the 1980s' (*Unemployment*, p. 61; p. 59).

In this context Hayek was willing to offer quite explicit proposals for reform. These included the end of all picketing in large numbers, the end of the closed shop, and the ending of exemption from legal liabilities arising from union action. However, Hayek argued that this package was not antiunion, but was opposed only to illegitimate (but currently legal) forms of union action. Workers would continue to have the 'right' to combine, and the 'right' to strike (except perhaps in essential services). Unions would still have a role in negotiating trade-offs between wages and conditions in firms, and in negotiating job hierarchies and other parts of the rules needed efficiently to run large organisations. In addition, unions could revive their 'friendly society' functions, which have been eroded by the welfare state, including the provision of sickness, injury and other benefits. However, a union role in management, 'industrial democracy', is undesirable. Such syndicalist ideas cannot work, as firms cannot be run in the interests of both workers and consumers, and such union management would detach union members from those who took on management roles, who would therefore cease to be proper representatives of employees (*Constitution*, pp. 276–7).

Hayek's account of the 'privileged' legal position of trade unions is challengeable on a number of grounds. First, his obsession with the 1906 act is misplaced. If one wants to give an account of the 'unique privileges' of British unions, then the 1871 Trade Union Act would be the logical starting point, because it exempted unions from the common-law doctrine of restraint of trade, which is the beginning of lawful trade unionism (Wedderburn, 1989, pp. 5–6). More importantly, the 1906 act was certainly not the unambiguous pro-trade union act Hayek suggests. Neither it nor successor legislation established any positive right to strike in Britain, unlike other Western European countries, so that all strikers remained in breach of their contracts of employment, for which they could be dismissed and be liable for damages (Wedderburn, 1989, pp. 4–5).

Second, the 1906 act was eroded over the succeeding decades by the inventiveness of judges. As noted in Chapter 2 above, the law on industrial relations is a good example of the limits of the rule-of-law doctrine. Judges, especially in the 1960s, outflanked the 1906 act, which gave unions immunities regarding breach-of-employment contracts, by allowing claims for damages for inducing breach of *commercial* contracts by industrial action, and by creating the new tort of intimidation out of the threat to strike itself (Wedderburn, 1989, pp. 6–7). A cynic might note that these erosions of the principles of 1906 came about when full employment tilted the balance of power in the labour market towards labour – unlike the inter-war period when the balance lay on the other side.

Hayek is undoubtedly right that many judges have not liked the 1906 and later acts, which give broad immunities to trade-union officers, seeing these acts as 'intrinsically repugnant to anyone who has spent his life in the practice of the law' (Lord Diplock, cited in Wedderburn, 1989, p. 7). But judges have been far from powerless in this area, so that Hayek's idea that unions in Britain have had all they ever wanted from the law is far from the truth.

Equally unacceptable is his assertion that unions have 'unique privileges'. This completely ignores the great privilege of corporations in being able to claim limited liability. Hayek accepts that this limitation is a privilege (*Studies*, p. 306) but nowhere discusses it in relation to trade-union immunities and their alleged uniqueness. This point has wider ramifications. Much of Hayek's attack on trade unions is couched in terms of the harm to society of group or collective selfishness as opposed to the benefits of individual self-seeking (*Law*, vol. III, p. 90). Why does this point not apply to corporations with *their* legal privileges? The answer is, of course, that in a developed capitalist economy the organisation of production requires such privileged entities to be granted the ability to pursue their own 'selfish' ends; otherwise complex forms of economic production might be unsustainable. The debate, reasonably enough, is not about how to abolish such corporate self-seeking, but how to regulate, channel and contain it. A similar point could be made about trade unions.

Hayek's analysis of trade-union activity starts from the assertion that most of this activity is geared to forcing the unwilling to join. This is simply untrue. Most strikes in Britain are about pay and conditions (*Department of Employment Gazette*, 1990).

Hayek's analysis of the impact of trade unions on the labour market assumes what labour economists call the monopoly model of trade unions. In this view the firm is always on its production-possibility frontier, i.e. producing as much as it can with existing technology. The demand for the product generates a demand for labour which is fixed and downward-sloping – i.e. the more labour is employed, the lower has to be its price, the wage. The monopoly view then simply notes that in this model, the only way a higher wage can be obtained is by restricting labour supply and thus getting higher wages at the expense of a fall in employment. Few modern labour economists would now accept this as an adequate account of the labour market. (For a survey see Oswald, 1986.) Unions, to very varying degrees, are sensitive to the employment consequences of their actions. In some cases, e.g. where they have members amongst the unemployed as well as the employed, this has had notable effects on their wage-bargaining behaviour (Newell and Symons, 1986).

More radically, some recent discussions of trade unions question the assumption that unions adversely affect productivity. The American economists Freeman and Medoff (1984) have argued that unions tend to encourage workers to voice their discontent, reducing labour turnover and promoting worker–management co-operation. This leads to enhanced productivity in union firms. Whilst Freeman and

Medoff's work remains controversial, most labour economists would accept that the old account, as given by Hayek, of unions as obviously productivity-reducing is far from clear (e.g. Hammermesh and Rees, 1988, ch. 11).

Finally, on this aspect of unions, the monopoly model assumes that union presence will have a significant impact in raising the level of wages of the unionised compared with the nonunionised firm. Again, whilst this remains a controversial area, the evidence of a significant impact from unionism *per se* (as opposed to things which may correlate with unionism, e.g. size of plant) is thin. Some recent studies suggest the average impact is well down in single figures (e.g. Blanchflower, 1986).

A view that unions have limited effects on wages would obviously carry the implication that the impact on unemployment via distortions of the relative wage structure is also limited. Hayek's discussion of the union–unemployment link focuses on the 1970s and 1980s, and for this period few studies of the causes of unemployment give much weight to trade unions (Layard and Nickell, 1986).

Hayek's view that trade unions force governments into inflationary policies by insisting on full employment at any money-wage level seems equally unpersuasive. The full employment policies of the post-war era, whilst obviously supported by trade unions, were based on a political commitment by successive governments to 'high and stable' employment, as embodied in Britain in the 1944 White Paper, *Employment Policy*, and on similar policies in other advanced countries. This commitment undoubtedly imparted an inflationary tendency to the price level over the post-war years, but the surges in inflation of 1950–2, 1972–4 and 1979–80, were not the result of trade unions insisting on the financing of particularly inflationary wage settlements by expansionary macroeconomic policy, but were largely caused by sharp increases in international commodity prices (see the sections on Full Employment and Inflation in this chapter above).

Unions have undoubtedly been part of the inflationary process in the post-war period, but their role has been much less central than Hayek suggests. The major aspects of that process have been tight labour markets and generally expansionary economic conditions. Unions have been more in the nature of transmission mechanisms for forces arising elsewhere, than major originators of the inflationary trend.

To see trade unions as the key to Britain's relative industrial decline is equally implausible. This decline is, of course, an enormous subject with an enormous literature. But from whatever part of the spectrum of opinion writers on this topic came, practically none would see unions as having a primary role, as opposed to, at most, a contributory role. Thus even violently antiunion writers like Barnett (1985) rate the failings of education and training well ahead of trade unions. More 'mainstream' writers (e.g. Crafts, 1988) similarly can find only a limited role for unions. Once again Hayek seems to have engaged in gross rhetorical excesses as part of his contribution to the 'moral panic' over economic policy in Britain in the 1970s.

Hayek presents himself as a supporter of trade unions in their 'proper' role – including conceding a right to strike. Yet this is combined with proposals to withdraw all immunities from trade unions in respect of such strikes. It is difficult to see how these positions can be compatible, as, in the case of Britain, with no immunities unions and their organisers would be open to the whole weight of the law of tort, with the potential losses in damages making strike action financially catastrophic for unions. Of course, if the current immunities were to be replaced by positive rights, as in most continental European jurisdictions, the matter would be different – but Hayek does not advocate this.

Hayek's case for 'legitimate' trade unionism certainly does not embrace any notion of industrial democracy. His main point against it is the traditional argument against syndicalism – that it privileges the interests of producers against the interests of consumers. The problem with this argument in its general form is that it ignores the fact that firms are inherently decision-making and strategic entities, i.e. they are never simply reactive to signals from consumers, as much orthodox economics implies, but pursue their objectives within a variety of constraints, including those imposed by consumer demand. Hence the claim of industrial democracy is not, of course, that consumer interests shouldn't count in the firm's decisions, but that workers should have a major say in firms' strategic decisions. If 'democratic' firms exist in a system of (regulated) competition, there is no reason to assume the simple interest clash of producers versus consumers that Hayek asserts.

Industrial-relations law is an area where the influence of Hayek has been divined behind British policy since 1979 (Wedderburn, 1989). In successive acts since 1980 the immunities and capacities of unions have been narrowed, very much along the lines suggested by Hayek, until the possibility of any legal strike action had come into question by the end of the 1980s. Yet the result of all this has definitely not been to have transformed the workings of the British economy, as Hayek's analysis suggests it should. Inflation, including wage inflation, is still high by international standards. Manufacturing productivity has improved since the 1970s, but there has been no 'miracle', and Britain remains unable to finance its import bill from exports at anything like a full-employment level of output. The British disease has not been cured. (For a summary of the economic results of the Thatcher years, see Tomlinson, 1990, ch. 11.)

Finally, Hayek's failure to deal with the basic case for trade unions may be noted. Only in a footnote does he deal with the issue of equalising the differences in bargaining power which are commonly seen to lie behind the legal fiction of equality that, in turn, lies behind the contract of employment. Hayek writes:

> Whatever limited validity the old argument about the necessity of 'equalising bargaining power' by the formation of unions may ever have had, it has certainly been destroyed by the modern development of the increasing size and speci-

ficity of employers' investment, on the one hand, and the increasing mobility of labour made possible by the automobile on the other (*Constitution*, p. 506, footnote no. 9).

It need hardly be said that such a view of the labour market scarcely matches the 1980s reality of high unemployment and overstocked labour markets, coupled with the relative immobility of many workers (especially married women) and the growth of jobs in low capital-intensity service sectors. In such a situation inequality of bargaining power, and hence the basic case for trade unions, appears only too prevalent.

Conclusions: The Erosion of Freedom?

For Hayek, the development of the post-war managed economy and welfare state was the culmination of the trends away from freedom, apparent in the rise of collectivism from the late nineteenth century (here Hayek closely follows Dicey [1914]). The post-war consensus takes the Western world a long way down the road to serfdom.

As we have seen in this chapter, many of Hayek's specific predictions about the developments of the post-1945 period have been wrong. But what about the key issue of freedom? As noted in Chapter 2, Hayek's freedom is essentially quantitative, and whilst he does not attempt any such assessment, it is possible to sketch such an assessment as Wootton (1945) did in responding to Hayek's *Road*, largely sticking to his definition of what is to count as freedom.

Following her list of freedoms, the first to be considered are what may be called 'economic' freedoms. Freedom of consumers to spend their income on what they will remains unaltered in all significant ways. More problematic is consumer sovereignty – the freedom of consumers to determine what is produced. Here there has been an erosion *if* one treats consumer sovereignty as represented only by market mechanisms; a greater share of the national product is spent by government than was the case before the welfare state.

But even within this framework two points are worth stressing. First, the share of government spending in the GNP rose much less in this period than many in the 1970s, including Hayek, suggested. Rather than this share reaching 60 per cent (*Denationalisation*, p. 57), on the standard international measure it rose in Britain to only 47 per cent at its peak in 1975. Other Western European countries recorded a similar figure (Heald, 1983, pp. 29–32). Second, most of the rise was due to transfer payments, i.e. taxing the income of one set of households to finance the expenditure of others. Governments obviously had to tax to do this, but they did not determine what the money was spent on, leaving this to the recipients of the transfers.

All this assumes that the rise of the state's role is equivalent to the erosion of freedom. But there is good evidence that this pattern of expenditure reflects consumer choice. For example, Taylor-Gooby (1985) shows how the principle of welfare provision by the state is popular amongst British voters in this area; in other words the political market place works in giving consumers what they want.

A crucial freedom for Hayek (and rightly so) is freedom of choice of employment. It would be hard to argue that this freedom has been eroded under the welfare state – indeed the principle of reducing arbitrary exclusion from employment has been extended (however inadequately) by the enactment of the Sex Discrimination and Race Relations acts in Britain, and by parallel laws in many countries which have extended this principle. There has been no move to use the expansion of state-financed services as a way of politically discriminating in the labour market.

Equally 'freedom of enterprise' – the capacity to set up and run businesses – was only marginally affected by the post-war nationalisations, which at their peak still left at least 80 per cent of output in private hands in all Western European countries (ignoring here the privatisations of the 1980s). Whilst the higher taxes of the post-war period have eroded the wealth accumulations required to set up businesses in some sectors (though the extent of this should not be exaggerated – in Britain those in the top 5 per cent of the wealth distribution table still own 50 per cent of marketable wealth – Hills, 1988, p. 40), the number of businesses in existence continued to rise, even before the stimulus given by shifts of policy after 1979. If Britain has lagged behind the other capitalist countries in the number of its small businesses, this has reflected much more the operation of the financial system in that country than the expansion of the state (Bolton, 1971).

Finally, let us consider political freedoms in the broadest sense. Overall the picture is surely clear – no significant political freedoms have proved incompatible with the welfare state. The rights of voting, and the freedoms of assembly, speech, and thought remain largely unaltered. At the edges some of these may be under pressure; e.g. the British Public Order Act of 1986 puts limits on the freedom of assembly which are potentially dangerous. More worrying in recent years has been the erosion of checks on government powers. In Britain the secrecy of government, its desire to suppress civil-service dissent at government malpractice, and the centralisation of power in Whitehall have all been features of the years of Conservative government since 1979 (Gamble, 1988). Two points may be made about this process in relation to Hayek's arguments.

First, this process has gone on whilst the directly economic activity of the state has been reduced, not, as liberals like Hayek have suggested, as a consequence of a growing state role.[5] Whilst, as noted in Chapter 2, Hayek's thesis that a fully state-controlled economy is incompatible with many important freedoms may well be acceded to, this does not imply that there is some straightforward general relation between the economic role of the state and political freedoms. The liberal economy and the authoritarian state is an only too prevalent combination.

Second, this combination brings out a major 'strategic' shortcoming of Hayek's approach. By basically arguing for a return to the golden age *before* the rise of the welfare state, he evades the task of formulating programmes for more effective scrutiny and accountability of 'big government'. Calling for a return to nineteenth-century forms of government is little help to those seeking to control the realities of late twentieth-century government. (On this theme, see Chapter 6 below.)

Notes

1. On other issues Hayek differs significantly from Friedman. Two of these are noted in the text of this chapter, but there is also a wider methodological difference between the two. Friedman is much closer to the 'scientific' macroeconomics tradition that believes in the importance of economic measurement and hypothesis-testing, which Hayek's Austrian approach strongly disagrees with.
2. For general critiques of this approach, see Toye (1976), and for the broader rational choice approach to human action on which it rests, see Hindess (1988).
3. This is not to say that Keynesianism, in so far as it contributed to the full-employment commitment, was wholly unimportant. That commitment was important in ruling out severely deflationary responses to post-war balance-of-payments problems, and hence probably encouraged private investment, as well as in contributing significantly to the open international economy under the Bretton Woods/GATT arrangements.
4. For such amenities Hayek favours local provision wherever possible. This allows people to choose among different levels of provision by moving location.
5. The concept of the economic role of the state is treated here in a conventional fashion. In Chapter 6 the conceptual issues involved in this conventional approach are discussed, above all the *redefinition* of 'the economy' implied by much recent conservative policy, especially in the British case.

5

Hayek and Socialism

The counterpart to Hayek's attempt to refound the bases of liberalism has been a lifelong concern to attack socialism. The focus of that attack has varied, but it has been little interested in Marxism or communism. Much of the attack has therefore been on varieties of democratic socialism. Central to that attack has been the argument that socialism is unacceptable not because of its values, but because of its intellectual errors. Socialists are wrong not because of their malevolence or bad faith, but because they do not understand the implications of what they argue for. Socialism is 'a mistake' (*Fatal*, Introduction) grounded on a misunderstanding of how societies work. This mistake has many facets and implications, but at its core is a misunderstanding about how economic systems work.

> The main point of my argument is, then, that the conflict between, on one hand, advocates of the spontaneous extended human order created by a competitive market, and on the other hand those who demand a deliberate arrangement of human interaction by central authority based on collective command over available resources is due to a factual error by the latter about how knowledge of these resources is and can be generated and utilised (*Fatal*, p. 7).

Economic Calculation and Socialism

Hayek's critique of socialism has ramified through almost all the issues he has written about – economics, law, epistemology, political philosophy, ethics – but its starting point in a chronological sense, and its mainstay has been a critique of central direction of economic activity. His first published work in this area was in the 1930s, in the context of what came to be called the economic-calculation debate of those years. This debate revolved around the question of whether a centrally planned economy, as then advocated by many socialists, could be successful. Hayek's role in this debate was to edit and comment upon a collection of Continental essays for an English-speaking audience (*Collectivist*), and in doing so to participate in a debate which engaged much academic opinion in the 1930s, and which is of central importance to our understanding of how economies can be organised.

In his introductory chapter to *Collectivist* (reprinted in *Individualism*, ch. 7), Hayek outlined his perception of the 'Nature and History of the Problem'. He stressed the lack of discussion amongst socialists of the nature of a socialist economic system. He saw the acceptance of the superiority of a socialist economic system as being based on a common but poorly argued trend to believe that deliberately regulated systems are superior to the unregulated, apparently haphazard operations of the market. Hence a better understanding of how a market system works would provide a powerful critique of the little-elaborated desires of socialists for a replacement of that system.

Hayek has written strikingly little on Marx, unlike other Austrian economists like Joseph Schumpeter.[1] But one key element in his case against economic planning is that Marx and his followers were wrong to suggest that the phenomena of economic life are related to the different phases of economic development in history. Against this view he asserted that there is *the* economic problem, 'the general problem which arises everywhere when a multiplicity of ends compete for a limited quantity of means' (*Collectivist*, p. 24).[2]

For Hayek, this problem, i.e. how inherently limited means could be allocated amongst competing ends, is successfully solved in a competitive market system by the unplanned interplay of the demands of consumers and the production decisions of producers. The value of goods produced in such a system is the consequence of their evaluation by consumers, and producers strive to match their outputs to these evaluations in order to make a profit. The central question for a socialist economic plan would be the problem of 'value', i.e. how the plan would evaluate goods, and hence how it would make decisions on what to produce. How could such decisions be made without the evaluations placed on consumer goods in the market for such goods, and evaluations of producer goods by entrepreneurs?

The key author on this subject, according to Hayek, is the Austrian economist von Mises. In his article 'Economic Calculation in a Socialist Community' (reprinted in *Collectivist*, ch. 3), von Mises's central argument is that in a socialist community a market for consumer goods alone will not make rational economic calculation possible. The key problem for such a community is the evaluation of producer goods: 'That can only be done with some kind of economic calculation. The human mind cannot orientate itself properly among the bewildering mass of intermediate products and potentialities of production without such aid. It would simply stand perplexed before the problems of management and location' (von Mises, *Collectivist*, p. 103). For von Mises, rational decisions on what and how to produce can take place only in a market system with private property, which allows each individual to evaluate consumer and producer goods and transmit those evaluations to others by the price system. Socialism, defined as the collective allocation of producer goods without the benefits of such evaluation, is, then, 'the abolition of rational economy' (*Collectivist*, p. 110).

For Hayek, von Mises's argument was decisive in showing that a combination of central direction of all economic activity and the absence of private property could not produce an output comparable to that produced under free competition. In his concluding essay in *Collectivist* (reprinted in *Individualism*, ch. 8), entitled 'The Present State of the Debate', Hayek attempted to reinforce this conclusion by looking at the results of the Soviet Russian experiment in economic planning, and then at the socialist responses to attacks on the possibility of economic planning.

In his brief comments on Russian planning, Hayek relies heavily and explicitly on the work of Brutzkus (1935). The argument from Brutzkus is that Russian planning has produced a low level of consumption, lower than would have been the case if Russian capitalism and free competition had continued in combination with the level of savings actually achieved in the Soviet period. Equally, the basic irrationality of Soviet planning had been exposed, first by the abandonment of war communism in 1921 and the partial revival of markets under the New Economic Policy, and then by the difficulties of realising the famous five-year plans of the late 1920s and early 1930s (*Collectivist*, pp. 203–7).

In his discussion of socialist economists' reactions to the attack by von Mises and others, Hayek first of all emphasises the sheer scale of information which a central plan would have to incorporate to replicate the workings of a capitalist system. In particular he stresses that every machine or tool is different in its state of wear and tear, its location and so on, and it will therefore have to be treated as different from every other machine or tool, and consequently will have to enter separately into the calculations of the planning authority (*Collectivist*, pp. 208–10). On top of this he argues that much of the technology of production is constantly developing by *small* changes, so that the plan would have to take this into account, i.e. know about all these constantly changing possibilities as well (pp. 210–11).

Even if all this information was accumulated by the planners, Hayek argues, to formulate a plan would require the solution of a set of equations equal in number to the number of different commodities to be produced: 'At present we can hardly say what their number is, but it is hardly an exaggeration to assume that in a fairly advanced society, the order of magnitude would be at least in the hundreds of thousands' – hence the project is 'utterly impracticable' (*Collectivist*, pp. 212–13).

Hayek's comments on socialist economists focus on those who responded to such arguments against traditional socialist planning by advocating a form of socialism in which markets for labour and all goods exist, but property is owned collectively and run by salaried managers aiming not at profit but at covering costs. As Hayek notes (*Collectivist*, p. 219), such schemes

> raise the question of the *rationale* of private property in its most general and fundamental aspect. The question, then, is not whether all problems of production and distribution can be rationally decided by one central authority but whether decisions and responsibility can be successfully left to competing individuals who are not owners or are otherwise directly interested in the means of production under their charge.

Hayek's answer is that under such a system there will still be fundamental problems about what amount of resources each enterprise is to be granted use of. There will be a constant tension between, on the one hand, letting managers take risks with resources and, on the other, the centre trying to plan, in a world of constantly shifting circumstances. There would be a division in the power over disposition of resources which would make it difficult for anyone to plan and would make it impossible to assess responsibility for mistakes in such dispositions. Attempts to have markets in combination with an absence of private property would therefore be no more plausible than those based on complete central economic planning, and, Hayek argues, such schemes do not contradict the conclusion that 'to-day we are not intellectually equipped to improve the working of our economic system by "planning" or to solve the problem of socialist production in any other way without very considerably impairing productivity' (*Collectivist*, p. 241).

In his final major contribution to the debate, in 1940 (reprinted in *Individualism*, ch. 9), Hayek asserted that the arguments over the possibility of an economically rational socialism had gone through three stages. The first had been the refutation of the view that socialism could dispense entirely with calculation in terms of values and replace it by some calculation of physical magnitudes, for example, labour or energy. The second stage had been the refutation of the view that the central planners could replicate the workings of a market by gathering all the relevant information and solving the equations, employing the method of trial and error to adjust the plan subsequently. This 'mathematical solution', as Hayek labelled it, had, he believed, been decisively refuted by the Italian economist Pareto (*Individualism*, pp. 181–2). The third stage was the discussion of the 'competitive solution' already noted above, of combining public property with competitive market relations. The purpose of Hayek's 1940 article was to develop the critical points made in the 1935 book, especially in the light of two well-known books advocating this kind of socialism, by, respectively, Lange and Taylor (1938) and Dickinson (1939).

The broad thrust of Hayek's argument in the 1940 article is the same as previously, but one element in particular is emphasised, and this is of crucial importance to Hayek's whole position on socialism. Having made the point about the unstable division of responsibility between the enterprise manager and the central planners, Hayek goes on to stress that the key problem is the nature of the decisions that enterprise managers will be faced with. Rather than being faced with a choice among objectively costed techniques,

> the method which under given conditions is the cheapest is a thing which has to be discovered anew, sometimes almost from day to day, by the entrepreneur, and that, in spite of the strong inducement, it is by no means regularly the established entrepreneur, the man in charge of the existing plant, who will discover what is the best method (*Individualism*, p. 196).

For Hayek, the debates about economic planning and socialism were settled decisively in the 1930s. Much of his own work in later years, can, however, be seen as developing from the issues raised by this debate. The most immediate issue was the character of economic knowledge. Already in 1937, in 'Economics and Knowledge' (reprinted in *Individualism*, ch. 2), he argued that a key task of economics is to understand how order could emerge in a system characterised by fragmented knowledge; by what he called the 'division of knowledge'. In 1945, in 'The Use of Knowledge in Society' (reprinted in *Individualism*, ch. 4), he argued that much of the misunderstanding of economic issues is grounded on the inability to grasp the character of knowledge in society. Not only is this knowledge dispersed but its character is inherently particular 'knowledge of particular circumstances of time and place' (*Individualism*, p. 79) rather than objective, scientific knowledge. Hence the economic problem is how to adapt to changes in these particular circumstances, a problem which demands a decentralisation of decision-making, coupled with a knowledge of events in the wider economic system transmitted by signals from the market.

Hence, for Hayek, the key point in understanding how an economy operates is to accept

> the unavoidable imperfection of man's knowledge and the consequent need for a process by which knowledge is constantly communicated and acquired. Any approach ... which in effect starts from the assumption that people's *knowledge* corresponds with the objective facts of the situation systematically leaves out what is our main task to explain (*Individualism*, p. 91).

How compelling are Hayek's points about the irrationality of socialist economic planning?

First, he is surely right to say that at the time the debate began around the First World War, socialists had paid far too little attention to the organisation of a socialist economy, in part, as he says, because of the predominance of a Marxist hostility to 'Utopian' blueprints for the future.

But whilst this historical point may be conceded, its transient character is also apparent. Far from Hayek's implicit suggestion that socialists have refused to argue about the 'facts' of socialism and retreated into stressing their differences in values with liberals, there is a long list of socialist economists' contributions to discussion of the organisation of socialist economies which take note and build on the debates of the 1930s. This was true before the Second World War, for example, in the work of socialist economists like Durbin, Jay and Gaitskell in Britain (Durbin, 1985). Recent examples include, in the Eastern European tradition, the work of authors like Brus (1972, 1975), Wilczynski (1970) and Kornai (1971); more recently there is, for example, the important work of Nove (1983). All of these build on substantial knowledge of the workings of 'actually existing' socialism in the Soviet Union and Eastern Europe and are well aware of the kind of theoretical issues raised by Hayek and the other Austrians.[3]

These authors all accept that socialist economies *will* be faced with decisions about how and what to produce, which at the most abstract level are problems on a par with those faced in a capitalist economy. The idea that there is a general economic problem to be solved in all social systems is acceptable as a corrective to some socialist fantasies about an age of abundance, in which material scarcity will be abolished and there will be no economic problem to solve. (How far Marx showed such views, as often alleged, is debatable [Geras, 1985, pp. 81–5].)

This point made, however, it must be said that to talk of a general problem of matching scarce means to unlimited demands is both vacuous and harmful in the way it licenses certain economists' approaches. Vacuous because, except as a polemic against Utopian fantasies, it tells us precisely nothing about the range of economic institutions that may fulfil the function of allocation of resources. Harmful, because it leads much of economics to treat the character of human wants as datum, as given in some natural way, rather than as a crucial component of understanding the economy.[4] (On this issue see Hodgson, 1988, ch. 4.)

Of much greater interest is the controversial question of what exactly are the grounds of Hayek's case against central planning. The dominant interpretations of the calculation debate have emphasised what Hayek calls the issue of the 'mathematical solution', i.e. the problem of accumulation of such a volume of information by the planning agency as to make possible the solution of a set of equations to simulate in the plan the consequences of a competitive market. As noted above, Hayek, following Pareto, had emphasised, at one stage in the debate, the vast quantity of information required for such a task to be fulfilled, and talked of the project as 'impracticable'. This was not to say that it was theoretically impossible – as von Mises had 'loosely' stated (*Collectivist*, p. 36) – but that it would lead to a reduction in the average level of productivity in the economy if seriously pursued.

This argument is the one stressed by, for example, Schumpeter (1942, ch. 16) and Bergson (1967), who suggest that in an important sense the debate was a victory for socialist writers like Lange, Taylor and Dickinson who showed that, despite von Mises, rational socialist economic calculation was, *in principle*, possible. In this view Hayek's focus on the *practicability* of socialism was a retreat from the position taken by von Mises.[5]

But as Lavoie (1985) has persuasively argued, the line of argument by the antisocialists shifted little over the course of the debate. They responded tactically to different socialist arguments, but the basic thrust of the argument remained consistent. This thrust was not fundamentally about the *quantity* of information that central planners would have to handle, but about the *impossibility* of that information's being accumulated and used by central planners, given its character.

Lavoie, a sympathiser with Hayek's and the other Austrian economists' approach, rightly stresses that the position they argued for on central planning was part and parcel of an approach to the economy which was significantly different from that of the neoclassical economists, who, in fact, included both advocates of market socialism and commentators on the debate like Bergson and (in this context at least) Schumpeter. These neoclassicals viewed the competitive process as using a set of *given* information on prices and costs to arrive at an equilibrium; the socialists argued that this information could be effectively accumulated and deployed by the central planning agency. Hayek's and the other Austrians' argument was that this information is not objective, 'given' information, but subjective information, provided only in the course of competition and private ownership. As Lavoie (1985, p. 102) expresses the argument, 'the key point of the calculation argument is that the required knowledge of objective production possibilities without the competitive market process ... the requisite knowledge of the objective possibilities of production, can only be generated by a rivalrous process that pits different plans against one another.' In this view even the retreat from central planning to market socialism was unavailing because the latter still concentrated on the 'abstract formulation of optima at the expense of any consideration of the mechanism by which this aim might be realised' (p. 123).

Lavoie's work is very valuable in making clear the consistency of Hayek and the other Austrians in the arguments they deployed against socialism in this period. These arguments are also very much critiques of neoclassical economics, with its emphasis on markets providing a tendency to equilibrium, whereas the Austrians have always stressed that whilst markets provide some kind of order, their most important aspect is not so much that of allocative devices as a stimulus to entrepreneurship and economic progress.

In some respects this Austrian emphasis is more helpful in understanding a capitalist economy than the bizarre world of given costs and mechanical choice of techniques of much neoclassical economics. But to accept the force of the

Austrian argument in this sense is by no means to accept the whole Austrian account. Socialists can share with the Austrian economists an acceptance of the uncertainty and unavoidable ignorance within which economic activity must be conducted. Equally they can accept that production decisions require a knowledge of highly particular features of the environment in which an enterprise is operating. But what is needed, as Hayek notes, is to combine this with knowledge of the wider economy. For Hayek, this latter connection is made entirely by the price system – markets generate price signals which tell entrepreneurs what is happening elsewhere than in their own particular patch.

Hayek and the other Austrians, like the neoclassicals, argue that these market signals so determine economic agents' behaviour that the whole system tends to equilibrium, i.e. where all factors of production are in use and used for the maximum benefit. This argument is central to neoclassical economics, but, for Hayek and the other Austrians, it is an assumption which is qualified by their subjectivism, i.e. if economic agents react in highly idiosyncratic ways to their circumstances and market signals, why should the result be anything approaching an equilibrium? (Dow, 1985). In neoclassical economics, at least in the textbook versions, objectively correct knowledge is available to all agents and so there is no problem of how they will react as long as they are rational. This problem has in recent years split the Austrians into two camps.

> On one side are those who would minimise the importance of subjectivism and who stress the co-ordinative function of the entrepreneur. On the other are those subjectivists who question whether markets co-ordinate and who are now developing an alternative evolutionary framework, dubbed order analysis, to explain the workings of the market process (Caldwell, 1988, p. 530).

This divergence points to a fundamental tension in Hayek's work. On the one hand he holds to a belief in the traditional account of the efficacy of markets in co-ordinating economic activity, but couples this with his own stress on the 'division of knowledge' where that knowledge is always subjective, error-ridden and leads to plans inconsistent with those of other economic agents. This is just one area where Hayek, by pursuing an argument with characteristic rigour, regardless of consequences, undermines the simplistic conclusions which might be drawn from some of his arguments. Whilst it would be rather gross to claim that the tensions in Hayek's argument open the way to a role for economic planning in co-ordinating a subjective process, it is fair to say his argument does not rule out such planning quite so forcefully as it would if that subjectivism was tied to a convincing explanation of how it necessarily led to equilibrium. Without such a link Hayek may be said, in a paradoxical way, to have added to the weight of socialist criticism of the lack of automatic equilibrium arising from a market system.

Hayek's subjectivism is a useful counterweight to the world of technologically determined costs and 'objective' information assumed in much neoclassical theorising. Equally, the antiempiricism this subjectivism is embodied in – the emphasis on the irreducibly theoretical character of knowledge, that facts are never 'brute' – is persuasive against the epistemological crassness of much orthodox economics. In these ways Hayek's philosophical sophistication makes his approach far more enlightening than those of many of the standard economics textbooks. That said, however, his subjectivism remains extremely problematic.

As Hodgson (1988, p. 121) points out, 'In some respects all human agents are unique in their cognitive abilities and in the body of concepts they have acquired. Consequently cognitive theory does show that human knowledge has subjective elements. But if some of the *subject matter* of cognition is subjective, does that mean the entire process of cognition is subjective as well?' The answer, Hodgson emphasises, is no. He rightly stresses that cognition is not just a matter of individual psychology but is inherently socially constructed, not least because for cognition we rely on a language and linguistic structure which is socially formed.

The implication of these points is that whilst Hayek's subjectivism has considerable *polemical* force, it cannot form the basis of an adequate account of economic agents' calculations – the forms these take and the institutional frameworks in which they are embedded.

Thirdly, the Austrian account involves a veneration of the figure of the entrepreneur as the key player in the capitalist economy. The figure of the entrepreneur is often portrayed in counterpoint – for example, von Mises (*Collectivist*, p. 119) writes: 'The type to which the success of joint-stock companies is to be attributed, is not that of a complacently prosperous managing director resembling the civil servant in his outlook and experience; rather it is precisely the manager, promoter, and man of affairs, who is himself interested as a shareholder ...' This kind of dichotomy is endorsed by Hayek (e.g. *Constitution*, ch. 8), but is highly implausible. If we ask what makes for a successful capitalist firm, then it is far from clear that answers in these entrepreneurial terms will get us very far. Attempts to explain company success by the extent of manager shareholding have not been very successful (e.g. Scherer, 1980, pp. 34–41). The psychologism of contrasting 'complacently prosperous managing director' with the 'man of affairs' is crass in the extreme. More seriously, the whole approach of entrepreneurship ignores what have been helpfully called the 'national conditions of enterprise calculation' in shaping corporate behaviour (Williams et al., 1983, esp. ch. 1). In this approach the success or lack of it of enterprises is seen as crucially dependent on the forms of calculation employed by enterprises, which are seen as the product of a complex of institutional features – for example, the practices of the financial system, forms of accounting, and company law – not as the result of the presence or absence of 'entrepreneurship.'[6]

The point of this argument is not to denigrate what might be perceived as the personal characteristics of 'entrepreneurship', i.e. enterprise and drive. Rather, the point is to question the claim that entrepreneurship the mainspring of economic progress and the determinant of economic success, as claimed in Austrian economics. Socialists should certainly be in favour of enterprise and drive (amongst other characteristics) in individuals, but it would be an illusion to suppose any amount of these could compensate for the shortcomings of the structure of the institutions which create the framework in which enterprise functions.

Equally, to question the concept of the entrepreneur is not to question the importance of the search for technical advance in the economy, nor the fact that this is an inherently uncertain activity. But the point is that such advance arises in a wide range of institutional contexts which completely cut across the simple accounts of the antithesis between sclerotic, bureaucratic firms and entrepreneurial activity. A good recent case in point is the development of the transistor, the starting point for much recent technological change. This was originally developed in the USA by Bell Laboratories, a subsidiary of the giant AT&T with money from the US Defense Department. Only later did small firms like Texas Instruments and Fairchilds further develop and market the product (Auerbach et al., 1988, p. 75).

The idea of the importance of the entrepreneur is embedded in a broader conception of the market economy, the idea of the invisible hand. Simply put, this says that the pursuit of individual ends by members of a society can produce socially beneficial consequences *given* the appropriate framework. This idea is of fundamental importance to the debate over economic planning, because much of that debate involves the Austrian celebration of the beneficial consequences of individuals pursuing their own ends, against the planners' rejection of such an approach and belief that economic activity should be consciously regulated to achieve social ends.

Socialists' rejection of the invisible-hand argument has sometimes been based on its use to license all kinds of selfish and egotistical behaviour. But the originator of the idea, Adam Smith, and followers like Hayek, are perfectly clear that the argument presupposes a clear legal *and moral* framework within which individual objectives should be pursued, and that there is no presupposition that the goals of individuals are 'naturally' selfish, the key point being that individuals pursue their *own* goals, whatever they may be (*Constitution*, p. 78). So the argument cannot be so readily dismissed as some socialists imagine – it is not a celebration of the 'war of all against all'.

The invisible-hand argument has also been rejected as exaggerating the beneficial effects of individuals pursuing their own economic ends. As already noted in Chapter 3, many advocates of this idea have made hugely exaggerated claims for the general social benefits of the invisible hand; indeed, some of the claims seem essentially religious in character, on a par with 'God moves in mysterious ways his wonders to perform'. But with all the necessary qualification, socialists cannot entirely reject the invisible-hand doctrine. The economic-calculation debate has shown the limits to 'conscious control', to planning of the economy, a fact which necessarily implies allowing scope for unplanned economic activity and hence allowing the invisible hand (at least in part) to regulate this activity for the general good.

Acceptance of some form of the invisible-hand thesis does not, it must be emphasised, imply acceptance of a Hayekian general condemnation of planning. This general condemnation crucially relies not just on the invisible-hand thesis, but also on the assumption of fundamental incompatibility of markets and planning. For Hayek, there is no middle way between a planned economy and a complete reign of markets. This theme, whilst present in the economic-calculation debate, is developed much more in Hayek's later works and is of such importance that it is best dealt with at length in the next section of this chapter.

Whilst most of the economic-calculation debate was conducted at an abstract level, Hayek does suggest that the Soviet inter-war experience clearly demonstrates the failures of such planning and the unavoidable retreat from the attempts at full planning of the war communism period immediately after the 1917 revolution to the New Economic Policy of 1921 and then the allegedly incoherent 'halfway house' of the five-year plans from 1928 onwards.

In his discussion of Soviet-style economic planning Hayek argues that 'it was not the possibility of planning as such which has been questioned on the grounds of general considerations, but the possibility of successful planning, of achieving the ends for which planning was undertaken' (*Collectivist*, p. 203). But, in fact, the tests he applies do not do that; Soviet planning in the 1920s and 1930s was not primarily undertaken to raise consumption standards, as Hayek suggests. Rather, a primary aim was to build up the heavy industrial base for a combination of internal political (i.e. to build up the numerical strength of the working class) and external strategic reasons (i.e. to provide a defence against capitalist encirclement). It involves no necessary endorsement of these aims, nor the means used to achieve them, to say that to ignore this highly specific context is to give a wholly unhelpful discussion of Soviet planning in the interwar period.

Equally, it seems a little unhelpful to denounce Soviet planning of this period as wholly 'irrational' because of its reversals and changes of tack. Again, without endorsing what was done, we may say that it surely is unsurprising that the first attempt comprehensively to plan an economy was conducted on a trial-and-error basis, especially given the shift in objectives in the Soviet regime. This is not obviously evidence of irrationality, as Hayek alleges, but what today would probably be called learning by doing.

The Road to Serfdom and Beyond

The Road to Serfdom, first published in 1944, is Hayek's best-known work.[7] It is an unashamedly political polemic, called forth by what Hayek saw as the 'peculiar and serious feature of the discussions of problems of future economic policy at the present time, of which the public is scarcely sufficiently aware' (*Road*, p. v). The book is dedicated to 'the Socialists of all Parties' and the starting point of its argument is that collectivism, defined as the belief in central direction of economic activity, is now taken for granted across most of the political spectrum in Britain (and it is Britain that most of the empirical content of the book refers to, though the intended audience is wider and includes, especially, America). Hence whilst the polemic is against socialism, Hayek sees socialism as just the most politically important variant of collectivism, which could be used in pursuit of nonsocialist aims.

The themes of the book are twofold and interconnected. One is that socialism is on a par with National Socialism and other forms of fascism; that the prevailing intellectual and political climate in Britain mirrors that in Germany during and after the First World War; and, furthermore, that this climate is likely, if unchecked, to lead to the same disastrous consequences as in that country. The second thesis is that central direction of economic activity is incompatible with liberty, and that attempts to plan centrally the allocation of resources must either be given up or must lead inexorably down the road to serfdom.

The first theme is of course highly polemical and can be discussed more briefly than the second, which is of greater analytical interest. Hayek attempts to redraw the map of political argument, cutting across the normal Left/Right spectrum by suggesting that the great divide is really between individualism and collectivism, the latter having both Left and Right versions, but that these versions are united in much more than divides them.[8] There is both an intellectual and historical continuity between the two; the 'rise of Fascism and Nazism was not a reaction against the socialist trends of the preceding period, but a necessary outcome of those tendencies' (*Road*, p. 3). Intellectually, fascism and socialism have in common a desire to direct economic activity towards particular ends, whilst individualism is centrally concerned to provide a framework within which each person may pursue their own ends. For Hayek, such individualism has been at the basis of the growth of both liberty and prosperity, and both of these, but particularly the former, are incompatible with any form of collectivism.

Hayek's parallel between fascism and socialism is made apparently plausible only by a very selective account of socialism. Essentially what he does is to select from the complex and heterogeneous history of socialisms in all the European countries those examples of socialism which have involved a substantial degree of what may be called 'state worship' and thus have something in common with fascism. This focus on expanding the role of the state was clearly a strong and continuing element in much of German socialism; it was also characteristic of one important trend of British socialism, especially amongst the early Fabians and some of their successors in the 1940s. But it was far from typical of socialism in countries like France, Italy or Spain, where the pluralistic, decentralising element in socialist ideology has always been powerful. Even in Britain the socialism of the Webbs, H.G. Wells and many of the early Fabians has been paralleled by that of G.D.H. Cole and other advocates of industrial democracy and decentralisation of power. Indeed, for much of its history British socialism has been more akin to the advanced wing of liberalism than to the socialism of the pre-Nazi German Social Democrats (Crick, 1987; Wright, 1986).

The fact that in one important but specific regard there was a significant overlap between much of German socialism and Nazism tells us a lot about German politics, but rather little about socialism as a creed. That the Webbs' and H.G. Wells's enthusiasm for efficiency led them on occasion to some fascistic-sounding proposals is more a ground for questioning their socialist credentials than drawing wild conclusions about the character of socialism. As Eric Roll (1945, p. 179) wrote at the time in a review of *The Road*, in this part of Hayek's argument 'jejune analogies have to serve in place of real historical analysis'.

The thesis that economic planning threatens freedom is a

more lasting message of *The Road to Serfdom*. It was a message present in Hayek's earlier work – such as *Collectivist* – and it was to be a key theme in much of his later work. What distinguished the approach of *The Road to Serfdom* was its particular (and polemical) emphasis on the 'slippery slope' argument, i.e. that any attempt at central planning of the economy, however well-intentioned and apparently benign, could be rationally pursued only by greater and greater encroachment on liberty.

Hayek argues that central planning requires an agreement on ends which does not in fact exist. Whilst all can agree on the need to pursue the 'common good', when it comes to specific objectives, he argues, there is no such convergence of opinion. Hence the serious pursuit of specific ends must involve the reduction of democracy and the growth of coercion (*Road*, ch. 5). Control of the allocation of resources cannot be done without increasing control of individual lives, especially control of individuals in their role as producers (*Road*, ch. 7). The state as planner will no longer set the 'rules of the game' and be indifferent to the outcome of economic activity, but will have to favour particular interests over others (*Road*, ch. 6).

For Hayek, the problem could never be 'too much' planning because it was the very principle of planning which inevitably involved these consequences. The choice had to be between the market order and the planned economy. Hayek's position on this is worth quoting at length:

> The idea of complete centralisation of the direction of economic activity still appalls most people, not only because of the stupendous difficulty of the task, but even more because of the horror inspired by the idea of everything being directed from a single centre. If we are nevertheless rapidly moving towards such a state this is largely because most people still believe that it must be possible to find some Middle Way between 'atomistic' competition and central direction. Nothing indeed seems at first more plausible, or is more likely to appeal to reasonable people, than the idea that

one goal must be neither the extreme decentralisation of free competition, nor the complete centralisation of a single plan, but some judicious mixture of the two methods. Yet mere common sense provides a treacherous guide in this field. Although competition can bear some admixture of regulation, it cannot be combined with planning to any extent we like without ceasing to operate as an effective guide to production. Nor is 'planning' a medicine which, taken in small doses, can produce the effects for which one might hope from its thoroughgoing application. Both competition and central direction become poor and inefficient tools if they are incomplete; they are alternative principles used to solve the same problem, and a mixture of the two notions means that neither will really work and that the result will be worse than if either system had been consistently relied upon. Or, to express it differently, planning and competition can be combined only by planning for competition, but not by planning against competition (*Road*, p. 31).

This antithesis between competition and central direction of the economy lies at the heart of Hayek's work. By the time of *The Constitution of Liberty* in 1960 he could announce that socialism, in the old sense of common ownership of the means of production and in pursuit of 'production for use', not 'production for profit', was dead. From about 1948, he argued, it had been on a marked retreat across much of the globe (*Constitution*, pp. 253–6). But whilst the dangers of such wholehearted collectivism might have disappeared, the dangers of a drift towards socialism under the guise of the pursuit of social justice and by means of the welfare state remained. Hence the national economic management plus welfare-state 'middle way' that emerged in many Western countries after 1945 was, for Hayek, almost as great an enemy to liberty as the wholehearted collectivism that preceded it. The middle way was, for Hayek, no such thing but a large step down the slippery slope from freedom to serfdom.

Hayek's criticisms of the post-war social democratic consensus has been discussed in Chapter 4. But his thesis of an absence of any middle ground between a planned system and a market system requires a broader discussion not only because of its centrality in Hayek's work, but also because much other discussion on both Left and Right accepts this dichotomy.

Hayek follows much of orthodox neoclassical economics in treating 'the' market as an abstract principle, i.e. a mechanism which can be understood independently of the institutional framework that market is embedded in, or the calculations of the agents who participate in that market. The effect of this is to homogenise markets, to treat them all as on a par. Given this, it is logical to talk of a market 'system'; because markets are in essence the same, we can aggregate them without difficulty into a system. Such an approach is as characteristic of Marxist as it is of 'bourgeois' economics. The effects of markets are equally homogenised in both systems of thought, but in Marxism of course these effects – exploitation, alienation, commodity fetishism, capitalist anarchy – are portrayed as wholly bad rather than good. In similar vein, neoclassicals, Austrians and Marxists all see planning as a complete overthrow of the market principle, an effect desirable or undesirable according to political taste.

Because the plan–market dichotomy has been invested with so much political significance, rather few authors have challenged its analytical presuppositions, though many people, of course, have accepted the fact of the 'mixed economy' as a desirable mixture of planning and markets. (But one interesting challenge has come from Hodgson [1988, especially pp. 252–62], and his earlier work [1984, especially chs. 6 and 7].)

The alternative analytical approach would disaggregate markets according to the institutional conditions in which they operate and the forms of calculation participants in them employ. Thus, for example, the effects of financial markets would depend, amongst other things, on the legal status of financial companies (e.g. are they co-operative or profit-seeking), and on the character of their links with non-financial corporations (compare German patterns of inter-linkage with individual companies to the typical US and British separateness). It would also depend on the forms of calculation employed by those financial institutions – for example, are potential borrowers assessed on a 'going-concern' basis, or in terms of their worth if they cease to operate and their assets are sold off. (The importance of these points is brought out by Williams et al., 1983, ch. 1.)

What such disaggregation implies for political assessment of markets is clearly that great discrimination is required; the political desirability of markets which depends on their effects *cannot* be judged separately from the particularities of the market concerned. The same point can be made about the varieties of economic planning: its effects are not homogeneous, and cannot therefore be subject to a generalised political judgement.

Hayek's slippery-slope argument ultimately derives from treating markets and central economic planning as opposed principles, necessarily striving to displace each other. To oppose this difference as a principle is not to propose that plans and markets always coexist in perfect harmony. Far from it. But it is to propose that there is no mechanism which makes the survival of both within an economy impossible. The same point can be made in an empirical way if we look at planning in the capitalist economies in the post-war period. If we take the post-1945 Japanese case, we can see that planning in the sense of central determination of priorities in production has been successfully combined with competition *within* the sectors privileged by the state apparatus. Planning has been combined with competition, and in a manner which has been one condition of Japanese economic success (Johnson, 1982).[9] Equally, planning of major priorities in post-war France was not incompatible with a general policy of encouraging competition (Hall, 1986). This is not, of course, to argue that post-war planning has always been successful – this is hardly true of the British example (Hare, 1985). But the important general point is that planning and markets can and have been mixed in a variety of ways, ways that can be sustained without leading down the road to serfdom. This is a lesson we can legitimately draw from the experience of the advanced capitalist countries in the post-war period.

The Fatal Conceit?

In his most recent book (*Fatal*) Hayek returns explicitly to the polemic against socialism on which he has already expended so much effort. The book is based on a manifesto to be used by Hayek in a 'final showdown' with socialism. This intellectual gunfight at the O.K. Corral never took place, but its prospect led Hayek to summarise many of the arguments previously deployed in what his editor describes as 'a lifetime of doing battle with socialism' (*Fatal*, p. x). The major themes of the book are not new, though some receive greater prominence than previously, most notably the evolutionist argument and the implication drawn from it that socialism is incompatible with the existing levels of human population (see Chapter 3 above). Unfortunately, the basic paradox of this evolutionism, that history has allegedly 'gone wrong' with the rise of collectivism over the last 100 years, and yet that this has been accompanied by the most rapid population growth ever, supposedly the measure of evolutionary progress, is not resolved.

The Fatal Conceit also places great stress on, indeed derives its title from, the argument that socialists greatly exaggerate the capacity of reason to order human affairs. But Hayek does not go any further than before in making clear which reforms are legitimate, and which should be ruled out by their stemming from constructivist rationalism.

So after 50-odd years of polemic there remains a fundamental paradox at the heart of Hayek's account of socialism. By his definition that disastrous creed has advanced almost continuously since the 1870s, especially in Western Europe, and despite some reversals in the 1980s, it remains the case, in most of the advanced capitalist world, both that there is widespread belief in the traditional values of democratic socialism (BSA, 1989), and that the characteristic institutional consequences of that creed – big government, the welfare state, state intervention in resource allocation – remain largely in place. Yet for all their problems, these countries are more populous, more prosperous, than ever, and by most standards (including those of Hayek) freer than ever.

Notes

1. For Schumpeter, Marx was one of *Ten Great Economists* (Schumpeter 1952) whose work, especially *Theories of Surplus Value*, is a 'monument of theoretical ardour' (Schumpeter 1952, p. 21). Hayek, by contrast, crassly misunderstands Marx; for example, in suggesting Marx had no concept of a market economy's producing any sort of order (*Law*, vol. 1, pp. 69–70). Marx was of course well aware of the *imperfect* order of capitalism.
2. This definition of economics receives its most cited discussion in Robbins (1935, ch. 1).
3. Authors cited are those who are both theoretically informed and knowledgeable about the workings of actual socialist economies. Of course there are innumerable others who have written about socialist economies without possessing this combination of attributes to such a high degree.
4. Hayek discusses Galbraith's *Affluent Society* in *Studies*, ch. 23, focusing on the suggestion in that book that many modern wants are 'artificial' and therefore trivial. Hayek successfully shows that all wants are cultural artefacts and Galbraith's approach cannot be helpfully used to divide wants into 'important' and 'trivial'. But Hayek is unconcerned with how these cultural artefacts are produced: this is outside the domain of economic theory.
5. This view can lead to the idea that sufficiently advanced computational technology, modern computers, could solve the problem – a state of 'Computopia'. See Cave (1980, Introduction).
6. There is strikingly little critical literature on the notion of entrepreneurship.
7. It was commented upon by Keynes as follows: 'Morally and philosophically I find myself in agreement with virtually the whole of it.' His 'only serious criticism' was that Hayek gives no guidance on 'where to draw the line' and that he 'greatly

underestimates the practicability of the middle course'. Keynes's view was that we want more planning, but in conditions where as many as possible of the planners share Hayek's moral position (Keynes, 1944/1980, pp. 385–7). However, this rather misses the crucial point, that Hayek entirely rejects the *possibility* of a sustainable 'middle course'.
8. This idea of the fundamental political divide being between individualism and collectivism is not new to Hayek's *The Road*. It goes back at least to Dicey (1914). But it was given a new twist by Hayek.
9. But there have clearly been other conditions of Japan's success as a manufacturing producer, notably its form of enterprise organisation. See Friedman (1985).

6

Conclusions: Hayek at the End of the Twentieth Century

Hayek and Economics

Hayek occupies an ambiguous place in economic discussions. On the one hand many opponents of orthodox economics from the Left of the political spectrum see much merit in some of his arguments. In addition to the work of Hodgson, noted in Chapter 5 above, Auerbach (1988, p. 22, p. 23) has recently argued that Hayek is 'the most persuasive critic of the orthodox approach' to competition in the economy, and that 'Hayek's isolation in the academic world may be contrasted with how unexceptional his pronouncements seem to practitioners engaged in solving substantive, real world problems.'

The particular advantage of Hayek's approach that many antiorthodox economists see is his 'subjective' approach to costs, and the implications of this for how we understand competition. Hayek's approach is based on the view that costs are never objective 'facts' but are inherently dependent on entrepreneurs' expectations, as shaped by highly specific bits of knowledge about the economic environment. In his framework there is no place for the technologically 'given' costs of the static neoclassical production function. In Hayek's view the process of competition is always a process of discovery, of *overcoming* 'constraints' in factor and output markets, not just finding out and working within those constraints. In this area Hayek's arguments seem clearly superior to much of neoclassical theorising; certainly to much of that found in most economics textbooks.

However, Hayek's theories have the weaknesses of their strengths. Hayek's subjectivism is twofold. It involves postulating the subjectivism of the process of competition, but also the subjectivism in understanding that process. This latter view derives from Hayek's dependence on the work of von Mises, in which competitive behaviour derives simply from the assumption of rational action by individuals – this is known to us prior to and independently of any empirical work. This subjectivism as method is at the heart of Hayek's problematic status as an economic theorist. His attack on scientism (notably in *Counter-Revolution*) can be seen as a logical corollary to this subjectivism, ruling out the attempts by economists to ape the methods of the natural sciences. Hayek has not always been consistent on this point, as when in *Individualism* he refers approvingly to Karl Popper's *Conjectures and Refutations* approach to scientific method. In this work Popper proposed a general theory of scientific method by which theories were subject to a test of potential refutation. This involves some notion of 'objective facts' separate from the theories, a notion difficult to reconcile with the subjectivist method, which would deny the existence of objective information to use in such tests.

Put another way, Hayek's subjectivism would seem to make the possibilities of prediction of human action extremely limited. Whilst people in this framework may be seen as learning from experience, there is no *systematic* way they do so that would allow us to predict the effects of that learning on their behaviour. Ultimately, therefore, it is difficult to see how one can derive any conclusions about how an economic system as a whole functions from Hayekian assumptions. As Dow (1985) has persuasively argued:

> There is no theoretical necessity for individuals whose expectations have been disappointed to adjust their behaviour in such a way as to allow more rather than less co-ordination of their actions. The only possible solution is to focus all analysis on the subjectively determined behaviour of individuals, at the expense of reaching any aggregate conclusions. Where

such conclusions have been reached, the theoretical leap has been made of assuming that individuals' actions are co-ordinated harmoniously.

In other words, Hayekian economics cannot prove that market economies tend to equilibrium (e.g. full employment). Such a tendency cannot be derived from the subjectivist assumption about human action, and the subjectivist method would seem to rule out any empirical proof, or even any theoretical proof couched in traditional neoclassical economics, with its nonsubjectivist notions of knowledge.

A similar point can be made about Hayek's view of the macroeconomy. On one level he is hostile to the very notion of macroeconomics as a scientistic construct, which again ignores the inherently subjective character of economic behaviour. Hence, for example, his attack on the notion of 'the' money supply because it ignores the fact that what is accepted as money is inherently subjective – whether you accept my cheque may depend on your personal view of my trustworthiness. Despite this, Hayek has, of course, been both an analyst of the macroeconomy and a vociferous advocate of certain macroeconomic policies.

Prices, an analysis of trade cycles, was based on the assumption that cycles of activity result from the pursuit of inappropriate *policy* measures – excessive monetary expansion. The analysis shows how this wrong policy deranges the private economy. The assumption made, but unproven, is that in the absence of such public-policy errors the private sector could be stable. Such a presumption is equally at work with the advocacy of private money (*Denationalisation*) where to return the money supply to the private sector is to abolish money as any kind of economic problem.

Whatever may be the insight of Hayek into how economies work, especially in understanding the competitive process, the significance of this insight must be limited by the subjectivism in which it is encased. 'Indeed neo-Austrian *theory* does not provide a logical basis for an economist to advocate anything. It is only their quite separate confidence in market forces which justifies their policy statements' (Dow, 1985, p. 240).

Liberty

If Hayek had to be characterised in one phrase, it would have to be something like 'a philosopher of liberty'. Any summary assessment of his political and social arguments must, then, begin with his notion of liberty. As already emphasised in Chapters 2 and 3, Hayek's case for liberty is ultimately a utilitarian one; liberty produces the greatest possibility of the expansion of human numbers. Plainly, such a notion must at least give pause for thought when the sustainability of existing human numbers is open to question. And even if this ecological doubt is exaggerated, it is not obvious why human numbers should be regarded as the highest measure of the politically and socially desirable. Finally, as noted in Chapter 3, the whole emphasis on the growth of numbers is, for Hayek, embedded in an evolutionary schema which is, at best, ill-specified and highly controversial.

Requiring much more extended discussion are the intertwined issues of the definition of liberty, and the overriding weight given to this value in Hayek's philosophy. As noted in Chapter 2, Hayek uses and develops a traditional liberal notion of liberty as a *negative* value, as the minimal coercion of one person by another. It is thus explicitly *not* a 'substantive' notion of liberty, a notion involving a capacity of people to achieve any particular objectives.

> The question of how many courses of action are open to a person is, of course, very important. But it is a different question from that of how far in acting he can follow his own plans and intentions ... Whether he is free or not does not depend on the range of choice but on whether he can expect to shape his course of action in accordance with his present intentions (*Constitution*, p. 13).

The force of this argument for a negative definition of liberty has to be accepted, *if* it is counterposed to a simple positive substantive definition which links liberty to the attainment of human goals. The plain difficulty of such an alternative definition is that it easily collapses liberty into all the good things people may desire, and loses all specificity. More seriously, it licenses (negative) arguments that if freedom and liberty lead to hunger and deprivation it is better to be well fed and physically provided for even at the cost of all liberty of action – well-fed slavery is better than a hungry freedom. (The classic reference here is Berlin 1958.)

But Hayek's negative definition of liberty has its own serious problems. Whilst we may agree with him that it is nonsense to talk of a deprivation of liberty if our freedom of action is constrained by purely physical factors, his argument that infringement of liberty can result only from deliberate coercion by other people raises very serious difficulties. If the electorate in a democracy vote to pursue policies which have the predictable consequence of impoverishing a proportion of the population (e.g. by creating a sharp rise in unemployment), these unemployed, according to Hayek's view, are not coerced, because, individually, they were not the intended victims of the aims of others. But if, as Hayek rightly argues, responsibility can be sensibly talked about only in relation to actions which have foreseeable consequences, this unemployment *is* the responsibility of their voting behaviour (Plant, 1989, pp. 65–6).

Equally, if we use the same example, the rendering of some people unemployed and the reduction in income that results can sensibly be seen as a diminution of their liberty. To argue this point does not mean we have to *equate* liberty with income and wealth. Rather, it is to say that without a *minimum* level of resources a purely negative definition of liberty becomes meaningless. Again, this is not to argue that one should derive an argument for *equality* of income and wealth from arguments for liberty in a negative sense, as some socialists have tried to do. Rather, the case for equality has to be argued on its own grounds (see below). The point here is that one can argue that a negative definition of liberty can be sensibly combined with the notion that whatever benefits are said to derive from that liberty are likely to be absent without a minimum of resources – a minimum which will necessarily be related to the particular society under discussion.

If there are great dangers lurking in the notion of positive liberty, an adequate concept of liberty does entail rather more than simply the right to be left alone.

> But even our good negative liberties ultimately depend on positive political action ... People who use their liberty to avoid political life are more often done down than left in peace. The price of liberty is even higher than eternal vigilance, as Lincoln sadly said: it demands eternal action ... Liberty in this positive sense of public action does not deny liberty in the more liberal, negative sense of being left alone and in peace: it subsumes, complements and extends it (Crick, 1987, p. 86).

The dangers of a positive definition of liberty can, then, be reduced if we follow Wootton (1945, p. 9) in stressing that positive liberty is not omnipotence, the capacity to achieve all we desire, but a series of capacities for action which are 'definite, concrete, and always changing'.

A further severe limitation of Hayek's discussion of liberty is its emphasis on the state as the main agency of coercion in society. For him, the history of the last 100 years has been the history of 'men' using the state more and more to coerce others, and this type of coercion is the key target of his liberalism.

This approach raises two related problems. First, it offers a very restricted idea of the sphere of coercion. Perhaps most obviously, it links with a complete blindness about families. Hayek, like many conservatives, venerates the family (e.g. *Fatal*, p. 63) without, also like many conservatives, defining what he means by that term. This completely ignores the surely compelling evidence that families, in all their diversity, are extremely problematic in their implications for liberty in Hayek's sense, i.e. deliberate coercion of one person by another. Although he spells out his position remarkably little, Hayek presumably believes that if adults freely contract to enter a family (and can freely leave) there can be no coercion. But, of course, this ignores the inequalities between contracting parties in many families, as well as the fact that families are not wholly made up of freely contracting adults, which makes coercion only too frequent. Indeed the possibility of this coercion leads to the point that 'a major role of the welfare state is to protect individuals from their families' (Le Grand, 1989, p. 198).

A similar point relates to the typical capitalist corporation. For Hayek, as long as it is possible to leave one employment for another, no coercion by an employer of an employee can arise. Whilst it may be argued that the freedom to leave an employer and to find another *is* a key freedom, this does not satisfactorily deal with the general character of the employee relationship. If the choice is only between employment in similarly hierarchical and oppressive forms of organisation, then to some extent that choice is not a meaningful one.

The other point worth emphasising about both the family and the capitalist firm is that they are not, of course, spontaneous, natural growths but are themselves shaped by political and governmental action. This is commonly recognised in the case of the corporation, and Hayek himself briefly discusses the issue, though he fails to make the equation between the allegedly 'unique' legal privileges of trade unions and those of corporations (see Chapter 4). In the case of the family the point is less well recognised, but it needs to be noted that the meaning of 'the family' is (in part) the consequence not only of such obvious state actions as property, marriage and divorce laws but also of a whole series of governmental interventions in birth, health, child care and education, all of which seriously affect the content of what is meant by family life (see e.g. Donzelot, 1980; Minson, 1985, ch. 9).

This point about the family opens up a much wider issue – the whole way that the discussion is set up in terms of the role of 'the state'. Hayek is typical of much liberal and conservative thought in seeing a limitation of the power of the state as the key political task. The mirror image of this is the common (though far from universal) socialist desire to see the power of 'the state' expanded, especially in its control of private capital. Both sides of this argument depend upon a notion of the state as the site of power, benign or malignant according to taste. However, the terms of this debate can be challenged by challenging the idea of power that lies behind it. Power is seen here as the capacity of the state defined in a constitutional sense – the (written or unwritten) constitution grants certain powers to the state apparatus which it then deploys to good or bad ends.

Most obviously, such a view fails to register the *incapacity* of the state – the state is plainly not all-powerful, not sovereign in a world of footloose capital and multinational corporations. But more profoundly, such a view of power, it can be argued, ignores the fact that many of the forces which shape our existence and therefore 'have power', are not the emanation of 'the state', but of a complex set of institutions – schools, hospitals, asylums, universities, professional bodies, producer bodies, etc. In this view, whilst, as commonly accepted, the modern era is characterised by the growth of the state, that era is more fundamentally characterised by the rise of 'governmentality' – the rise of institutions and practices which seek to administer the lives of others in the light of beliefs about what is good, healthy, normal, virtuous, efficient or profitable. In this view the concept of power needs to be detached from its links with the constitutional/legal capacities of the state machine and linked to the capacities or, more exactly, *effects*, of this variety of bodies independent of the formal apparatus of the state.[1]

Such an approach to the question of power is not a panacea, but it does help to break up the 'individual versus the state' approach which often unhelpfully dominates the discussion of liberty. The political implications of such a critique are unclear; it has been used to support a facile libertarianism, where every social practice has a hidden and to-be-exposed power relation behind it, though this was certainly not the view of Foucault, an important advocate of this approach. But it would certainly undermine the Hayekian kind of liberalism in which the individual/state dichotomy is fundamental, and which completely fails to register either the problem of the historical specificity of what constitutes 'the individual', or the impact on social life of the myriad of institutions of the kind listed above.

Here Hayek is too much a captive of the historically determined discourse of liberalism. This historical component is especially apparent in the continuation into the late twentieth century of notions of the state's role in the economy directly following from those of Adam Smith in the late eighteenth century. Smith's well-known attack on much (though not all) state intervention in the economy was grounded in his appreciation of the corruption and malevolence of the state machine in his lifetime. But perhaps even more importantly, Smith wrote before the rise of most of the institutions which today shape our lives, so that his account of the state cannot be adequate to our understanding of power in today's 'liberal' societies.

Apart from the individual/state dichotomy, another reason why Hayek has so little to say about other social institutions is the notion of tradition. In his evolutionary schema, traditions have survived because of their congruence with evolutionary progress, and thus have proved their worth – little more need be said. But this raises obvious difficulties. As suggested in Chapter 3, such a scheme leaves it extremely opaque which precisely are the traditions which have contributed to progress – Hayek's evolutionary mechanism is underspecified. The only partial exception is 'the family', but the content of this and its contribution to evolutionary progress is not spelt out.

Concepts of tradition are often this vague: 'Tradition is no more than an umbrella term that designates an unspecified variety of controls, including internalised norms, that are not administered through public policy but somehow "spontaneously" through family, kinship, status and the like' (Lindblom, 1977, p. 13). Tradition, in the sense of largely unreflected norms of behaviour, is of course very important in understanding the possibility of social life. This should not be a point of dispute with Hayek. But his generalised veneration of tradition cannot help us understand which traditions do what, and hence which may be changed with what consequences. Yet this is precisely what we do need to understand for an adequate politics, a politics which does not treat its concerns as confined only to the public sphere of state action, but which is also concerned with aspects of the personal, e.g. familial life. The point is certainly not to propose that we 'start again' with a social life based on only those rules which can be fully rationalised in terms acceptable to all. This would indeed be a mad and probably politically catastrophic project. But this is not the only alternative to a veneration of tradition; we can, of course, make much more differentiated critiques of different traditions. This, of course, is precisely what Hayek does when he criticises the 'tradition' of a state monopoly of money issue.

Democracy

In Western Europe and North America today all significant forms of political argument are democratic in tone. Right-wing, antidemocratic politics was fundamentally undercut by the defeat of Nazism and fascism, and the experience of the Soviet Union and the rest of Eastern Europe seems, by the end of the 1980s, to have dealt a death blow to Marxism-Leninism as a significant alternative doctrine to parliamentary forms of democracy.[2] Within the spectrum of democratic politics Hayek occupies an extreme position – for him, democracy (i.e. majority rule) is probably, on balance, a good thing but it carries almost as many dangers as it does benefits. Majority rule provides a peaceful mechanism for changing rulers and for the political education of the majority (*Constitution*, pp. 107–9). But it holds great danger in that majority rule will be used to justify the suppression of liberty.

From a democratic socialist point of view such scepticism as to the value of democracy is salutary. It is a useful counterpoint to the often flabby use of the terms *democracy* and *democratisation* as if the effects of these were clearly beneficial. Linked to this is the usefulness of Hayek's limited meaning for democracy – a mechanism for selection of personnel to particular posts; again, this is a useful counterpoint to the only too prevalent habit of using *democratic* almost as a synonym for all the features of institutions we find congenial. Such an indiscriminate use of the term is not helpful to political understanding. Finally, as noted in Chapter 2, in broad terms Hayek's warnings of the potential dangers to liberty in a government able to claim majority support is hardly to be dismissed after, for example, more than a decade of Mrs Thatcher's rule in Britain or the uses made of presidential power in the USA in recent years.

These positive points made, however, there remain serious objections to Hayek's discussion of democracy. First the *scope* of democracy in Hayek's work is very limited. Most obviously, this is the case in his complete refusal of notions of 'industrial democracy' – of role for the employee in the government of enterprises. His arguments here are undeveloped and derivative, and largely depend on the idea that in a properly functioning market economy consumers' interests will reign supreme, and any kind of producer democracy will generate a producer interest group fundamentally in conflict with consumer interests (*Constitution*, p. 277).[3]

This argument is interesting on two counts. It assumes that enterprises could be simply the relays of signals from consumers to which producers simply responded as automata. Against this one can assert that whilst enterprises in markets do, of course, respond to signals from markets, these signals are always ambiguous in their implications for the enterprise. They always require the enterprise to *calcu-*

late a response, and in doing so to take all kinds of constraints and possibilities into account. The enterprise will, willy-nilly, have its own interests if it is a continuing organisation – the question is how its interests will be perceived and represented. Hence it is much better to think of markets as *constraints* on enterprise activity rather than as simple determinants of that activity. In this context some form of producer democracy adds a further element in the calculated responses and behaviour of the enterprise, rather than creating a simple consumer-versus-producer clash that was wholly absent previously.

Further, Hayek's dismissal of 'producer interests' is a case where he slavishly follows economic orthodoxy, an orthodoxy in which the social good is identified with the interests of consumers. But why should this approach be accepted when the role of people as producers shapes so much of their lives? Work is not only a 'disutility' compensated by a wage or salary, but also a central formative element in how most of us behave. It is also an area where we have a legitimate desire to improve our conditions, financial and nonfinancial. Of course we all benefit from low-cost production and cheap goods – but this is no good reason to make this consumer interest the defining issue in looking at how economies function.

Second, and more generally, Hayek's attack on industrial democracy is part of a general view that *any* politically influential interest groups are illegitimate and harmful entities, only existing because of the misguided actions of governments. This point was noted above in the discussion of Hayek's hostility to any form of 'corporatist' arrangements involving the political role of employer and employee interests (see Chapter 2). This approach is also evident in Hayek's complete lack of discussion of such intermediary institutions between the state and the individual citizen as political parties. In Hayek's preferred world it would seem that the only political actors are individual voters and the elected parliamentary bodies, their actions properly circumscribed by the constitution as enforced by judges.

Is this a plausible notion of political democracy? It does depend on assuming, first, that all intermediary bodies are essentially excrescences of the body politic, in existence only because of the monopoly-creating and harmful activities of government. This is surely not sensible. Even in a Hayekian economy the complex division of labour is going to create more or less long-lived bodies of, amongst others, workers and controllers of enterprises who will organise themselves and, more importantly, be able to make themselves felt. Effective government, however minimalist, will require the capacity to co-operate to some degree with these bodies. So an adequate account of democracy will have to include an analysis of how to come to terms with these bodies rather than their mere dismissal.

This issue is most pertinent in talking about large firms, the *political* actors, alongside parliaments and presidents, most important in almost all Western democracies. Here the words of G.D.H. Cole remain relevant:

> Individualism and laissez-faire quite change their practical meaning when the individual comes to mean in practice a great capitalist trust or a newspaper syndicate with unlimited capital at its back. It is useless to wish these giants away, or to sigh for the joys of an age of little things. There can be no peace for the soul of man, and no space for the individual to live his own life, till we have learnt by collective action to subordinate these monsters to our needs (cited Crick, 1987, p. 73).

Hayek's argument that the claims of majorities embodied in the notion of parliamentary sovereignty pose serious dangers to liberty is one to be taken seriously. The conclusion he draws from this is another matter. His answer to this danger is, on the one hand, to diminish the capacities of parliamentary majorities by superimposing an upper house which would enforce strict limits on the scope of government, and, on the other hand, to reduce greatly the size of government.

Leaving aside the eccentricity of Hayek's way of constituting the upper house (see Chapter 2, above) the key point is the kinds of rules which that house would impose. Plainly, for him, these rules would go far beyond the usual kind of constitutional rights regarding freedom of the person, and, above all, would exclude the possibility of abrogation of the rights of private property. But, as suggested above and as will be returned to below (see section on market socialism), Hayek's arguments on private property persuasively present the case for 'several' property, i.e. dispersed property ownership, but not *private* property in the traditional sense.

Rather more complex than Hayek's quite traditional conservative constitutionalism is the argument about the scale of government. Hayek is no advocate of laissez-faire (e.g. *Road*, p. 27) but it is clear, particularly in his discussion of welfare, that he envisages a huge reduction in the scale of government, especially in state spending. In Chapter 4 the arguments against Hayek's views on big government have already been put, and will not be repeated. The point in the current context is the rather different one of the *plausibility* of such a reduction in the scale of government, and what flows from this.

Plausibility must be a matter of political judgement, but the evidence of the 1980s would seem to suggest that even governments strongly committed to 'rolling back the state' will find it extremely difficult in the face of existing political conditions, most especially competition between political parties, to move back to small government. Even in countries where substantial privatisation has taken place in recent years – Britain, Australia and New Zealand, for example – this has largely left untouched state welfare expenditure (measured as a share of the GNP), which remains by far the largest proportion of total state expenditure.[4]

If this is the case, then there is a major issue about democracy. For, as Hirst (1986, 1989) has persuasively argued, the doctrine of parliamentary sovereignty has allowed, even facilitated, a lack of *any* control over much of the action of big government. Within modern big government

> the elected decision-makers are merely the short-term and largely unprofessional heads of a continuously operated administrative machine ... The policies of this complex of administrative agencies are largely self-initiated and self-regulated and the flow of information about them to members of the assembly and the public is closely guarded ... If I have said our system exhibits tendencies toward 'elective despotism' it is because so little detailed supervision or restraint is offered to executive power rather than that the executive power seizes on an unwarranted and illegal sphere of action (Hirst, 1986, p. 116).

In this view, a key issue of modern democracy is to find new ways to make state agencies accountable within the framework of representative assemblies. On this issue Hayek is the very opposite of helpful – he holds out the unrealisable (leaving aside undesirable) prospect of a return to government on the scale of the 1860s. Here Hayek offers us only nostalgia, not a plausible democratic programme for the late twentieth century.

Hayek's very limited notion of democracy is tied to the argument that it should be regarded primarily as a means rather than an end. In addition, for him, the ends which it produces are very limited – those of peaceful change in government; possibly, though problematically, the protection of liberty, and the political education of the populace (*Constitution*, pp. 107–9). The issue which his account raises is, should we consider democracy primarily as an end as well as a means?

Hayek's playing down of the importance of democracy as an end flows from treating liberty as *the* important political value. Against this may be counterposed the view that democracy should be seen as in itself an ultimate value on a par with liberty. This is not to ignore the possibility of a conflict between the two, nor to suggest that the results of democracy will always be congenial in other regards. There is a tendency on the Left to assume that democracy will always be favourable to causes the Left favours – for example, in arguments for democratising political parties or enterprises – an argument which, historically, seems hardly plausible. To argue for democracy or democratisation as an end in itself must involve accepting that sometimes its results will be unpredictable and uncongenial.

The case for regarding democracy or democratisation as an end in itself needs to be complicated slightly by arguing that the *substantive* results of democracy are never pregiven, but that the *procedural* aspects of democracy are themselves desirable. The point here is to accept but go beyond Hayek's point about democracy encouraging the political education of the citizenry. Beyond this we can argue for a 'republican' notion of democracy, a notion of an active citizenry involved in shaping the institutions in which they are involved. This does not mean assuming that the majority of the populace are thirsting to become continuously involved in every institution they relate to, but, equally, it is to argue against the notion of a passive citizenry which seems to be encouraged by a Hayekian notion of the meaning and limits of democracy.

As Crick argues in the quotation given in the previous section, the preservation of liberty requires an active citizenry, not simply appropriate constitutional mechanisms. But beyond that, socialists must not fight shy of saying they believe in active citizenship as part of the 'good life' they desire to bring about. This would apply to 'citizenship' of enterprises as well as of the state.

Equality

For Hayek, any policy of equality is fundamentally at odds with a free society. His argument is that material benefits in a market economy are not 'rewards' for effort in any sense, but the unintended consequence of a market order which allocates benefits by luck and chance as much as by contribution to output. Any policy based on notions of 'social justice' or equality, he argues, would involve the government's imposing a schema of just rewards, about which there could be no consensus, and which would involve *unequal* treatment of different individuals. In addition, he argues, if market prices for labour were no longer able to guide people into occupations, this mechanism would have to be replaced by state direction of labour and arbitrary decision by government (*Law*, vol. II, pp. 80–4).

The first point to be addressed is that of the extent to which material rewards cannot be seen as 'just' or 'unjust' because they are not the results of anyone's decision-making. Hayek argues:

> The prevalent demand for material equality is probably often based on the belief that the existing inequalities are the effect of somebody's decision – a belief which would be wholly mistaken in a genuine market order and has still only very limited validity in the highly 'interventionist mixed' economy existing in most countries today (*Law,* vol. II, p. 81).

The view of income and wealth distribution as being mainly the unintended consequence of 'the market' is plainly wrong. First, differences in current wealth holdings are very much the consequence of wealth inherited from the past, and acquired on the basis of all kinds of activity – from robbery to sex – as much as by any involvement in markets. Second, some of the major differences in income distribution – most obviously those between corporate directors and most employees – are very much the decision of those same corporate directors, who are largely immune from any shareholder or other pressure in today's oligarchical corporations. Third, it is quite plain that the distribution of income in today's mixed economies is very much tied up with government decision-making. For example, the Reagan government in the USA and the Thatcher government in Britain have very 'successfully' achieved a more inegalitarian distribution of income than existed when they came to power. In addition, as this was a known and foreseeable consequence of voting for those governments, it is a consequence that can be reasonably said to be a responsibility of those who voted for those political figures.

This is not to deny that 'market forces' determine that in Western countries today a computer programmer is likely to be paid more than a street cleaner. This is partly, of course, a consequence of the overstocking of the labour market with unskilled people, a consequence embedded, in turn, in the failure of the educational system adequately to equip the population with skills. Nevertheless, there is clearly some necessity to allow differences in income to act as a signal and incentive to people to change jobs and acquire skills as the patterns of demand and technology shift.

This is one of the areas where the 'slippery slope' style of Hayek's arguments is most apparent. For him, *any* attempt at deliberate regulation of the distribution of income must lead down the road to direction of labour and widespread coercion. But in fact governments can pursue a whole range of measures to make the distribution of income more equal, whilst accepting the need for some inequality and at the same time avoiding the consequences for freedom that Hayek alleges must follow such measures. Changes in the laws governing the ownership and functioning of corporations, changes in the pattern of state income maintenance, changes in the laws on inheritance, and greater progressivity in tax structures could all contribute to greater material equality without requiring either the assessment of 'merit' of particular individuals or the ignoring of the need for a functioning labour market. Estrin (1989, pp. 171–2) points to the successful functioning of the Mondragon system of co-operatives in the Basque region of Spain with their rule of a maximum income differential of 3 to 1 within a 'market' context. Despite Hayek's derision (*Law*, vol. II, p. 80), we can sensibly support the traditional socialist view that every departure from equality of material benefits has to be justified by some recognisable common interest which these differences serve.

Fraternity and Co-operation

Hayek's critique of social justice and egalitarianism commits him to the view that a market society does *not* reward merit: 'The values which their services will have to their fellows will often have no relation to their individual merits or needs' (*Law*, vol. II, p. 72). Conservative critics have argued that Hayek in making this point undermines the moral case for capitalism, which they see as based on the argument that effort and skill generate commensurate rewards (Kristol, 1971). Hayek recognises the strength of this argument, but, as elsewhere, is too honest to bend his arguments to arrive at a politically congenial conclusion. For Hayek, the moral case for capitalism or a market order can be only that it maximises the life chances, the chances of achieving the 'good life', of anyone selected at random, not that it produces any particular end result (*Law*, vol. II, p. 132).

This dispute raises a broad issue about how far Hayek's kind of capitalism is sustainable in the sense of how far it undermines its own moral and social foundations. This is a very long-running and widespread argument in the social sciences (Hirschman, 1977, 1982). Radical critics from Marx to Fred Hirsch, as well as conservative commentators like Schumpeter and Daniel Bell have argued that capitalism will 'self-destruct', partly because its competitive individualistic ethic will undermine the moral and communal ties, the social integration, upon which any society depends for its survival.

Hayek's view is not, of course, that a market society can exist independently of moral, any more than legal, rules. His point is that these rules must accept the restrictions of claims to morality and justice to areas where individuals can be held responsible for their conduct. Morality and justice simply do not apply to issues like income distribution. Equally, he is not an advocate of 'selfishness' as a virtue, but our capacity to be non-self-regarding, he argues, has to be accepted as limited – if we are altruistic towards everyone we are effectively altruistic towards no one. This, of course, is no more than the logical corollary of the strong version of the invisible-hand doctrine, wherein activity guided by individual ends, in a framework of appropriate moral and legal rules, yields the greatest society-wide benefit. The case against Hayek from both conservative and socialist directions is that this substratum of moral rules, which he well recognises the necessity of, will be undercut as the 'unintended consequence' of the expansion of the market.

It has already been argued above that Hayek's conception of the domain of responsibility and hence of moral conduct is too limited. In his version, moral conduct is limited to observance of abstract rules, in addition to altruism towards family and a close circle of known persons. But, as argued above, if we partake in, for example, elections which yield a foreseeable consequence for the welfare of others we share responsibility for those consequences, and our political actions are an appropriate object of moral assessment. Hayek avoids this point only by a grossly excessive estimate of how much things like the distribution of income and wealth are the consequences purely of 'market forces', and are outside any deliberate action.

On the other hand Hayek is surely right that there is something more than slightly ridiculous in attempting to make us all equally responsible for features of the world over which we can exert no control. The only consequence of this attempt to overgeneralise the domain of moral conduct can be to induce guilt, that most useless and disabling of emotions.

But Hayek almost certainly understates the extent to which emphasis by liberals on individualism and competition must tend to make altruistic and co-operative behaviour appear eccentric and perverse. This point, whilst important, must not be overplayed. However much the ideologies of capitalism have extolled individualism and competition, in practice even that most stereotypically capitalist institution, the profit-seeking firm, has always combined co-operative and competitive behaviour (Hirst and Zeitlin, 1989). Equally, as argued in Chapter 5, if we abandon notions of the fully planned economy (as we should – see also below on market socialism), then we have to accept some qualified notion of the invisible hand; we have to accept that there is no *necessary* contradiction between pursuing our own ends and the social good. This is another way of saying that all behaviour *cannot* be altruistic or wholly co-operative in a world of a complex division of labour.

The broad conclusion of this argument is that in the modern advanced economy there will always be complex mixtures of co-operative and competitive behaviour. Capitalism and its ideologies venerate the competitive and individualistic aspects – democratic socialists can reasonably lean towards the co-operative and altruistic, but should recognise the limits of both of these. In other words, socialists cannot be satisfied with the minimalist definitions of moral and fraternal behaviour offered by Hayek, but they do not advance their case by offering as an alternative an idea of society in which all actions are co-operative and directed to the immediate benefit of others; and in which the domain of moral and responsible conduct is so all-embracing as to be unattainable, and altruistic conduct so broad in scope as to be ultimately self-defeating.

Market Socialism

Whilst Hayek has emerged as a guru of the New Right in the 1970s and 1980s, his influence is not limited to those who share that political perspective. His arguments about the political implications of central planning have found some resonance on the Left, especially amongst those who for a whole variety of reasons have rejected the common identification of socialism with central planning. A notion like market socialism might be seen as drawing upon some Hayekian themes about benefits of the market, whilst attempting to combine these with traditional socialist political objectives, especially reducing the power of private capital and creating a more egalitarian society.

Market socialism is an ambiguous concept. If it simply

meant socialism with *some* role for markets, hardly any contemporary version of socialism would be excluded by such a definition. The key issue is to what degree markets play a role in a socialist economy. Here Hayek's arguments, whatever their influence on debate on the Left, are very important. For, in many ways, Hayek's views on the relation between markets and planning are the mirror image of those of orthodox Marxism and its advocacy of central planning. For example, Mandel (1986, p. 7) whilst using Marxist terminology, is saying nothing different in essence from Hayek when he declares that 'planning and the market are fundamentally different from each other ... essentially they have a different internal logic. They diffuse divergent motivations among producers and organisers of production, and find expression in discrepant social values.'

Mandel, like Hayek, regards planning and the market as incompatible principles, of which one must 'rule' and one be subordinate. Unsurprisingly, for Mandel, this means any notion of market socialism must be anathema – once the case for the market is conceded, socialism cannot survive as a coherent political idea. For him, economic planning is the essence of what is meant by socialism. Such a critique might reasonably apply to the work of *some* market socialists whose advocacy of 'the market' dominates socialist objectives (or makes 'liberty' the key objective, and in doing so takes on board most of the Hayekian baggage). This would seem to be the case in, for example, some of the discussion in Forbes (1986).

As already suggested in Chapter 5, the key issue here is the planning/market dichotomy, and some of the problems of that dichotomy are discussed in that chapter. Hayek's argument against central planning, it is worth reiterating, is basically an epistemological one – the incapacity of a central planning body to know what needs to be known, rationally to organise economic activity. In most contexts this may be granted some force as an argument against the idea of a single site of decision-making for a large economy. But this polarity of central/decentralised knowledge is ill-specified. Is the decentralised agent an individual or, alternatively, a large-scale, perhaps even a multinational, corporation? If the latter, how is *it* to agglomerate information whilst retaining the specificity of that knowledge? In what knowledge-gathering sense is a large corporation different from a central-planning agency? The crudeness of Hayek's dichotomy is especially evident in his key 1945 article 'The Use of Knowledge in Society', in which the centralised/decentralised polarity is allowed no gradations except 'the delegation of planning to organised industries, or, in other words, monopoly' (reprinted in *Individualism*, p. 521).

As elsewhere in his work, Hayek, in pursuit of his theoretical schema, provides strikingly little in the way of accounts of institutions. In the area of planning it means there is no attempt at discussion of levels of decision-making in an economy, how information has to be transmitted within organisations, and, hence, how the highly specific knowledge of those in a particular market must be aggregated together with other knowledge to a greater or lesser extent in organising economic activity.

Another issue in the Hayekian approach to information is the assumption that the market will provide signals in a form adequate for rational economic decision-making. But the information provided by markets is usually of a specific kind – it is about the current state of the world and it is in quantitative terms. But investment decisions, the crucial decisions made by enterprises, require information about the future and also about, for example, the problems of combining old and new technologies in a production process which cannot be represented in simple quantitative terms. Of course *no* information about the future is perfect – investment is inherently risky. But two points need to be made. First, Hayek's exaltation of the information-generating and -dispersing capacity of the market needs to be qualified by noting the limits of the *kinds* of information generated by markets. Further, we need to ask what kinds of institutions generate potentially superior forms of information – for example, for investment decisions.

One specific area where discussion on these lines has made a case for some forms of planning is in the area of indicative planning. Here even enthusiasts for market mechanisms can make a strong case for a form of planning which essentially aims to pool information and hence, to a degree, reduce uncertainty amongst producers and so encourage activity at higher levels than would otherwise be the case (Estrin and Winter, 1989, pp. 115–19). The point here is not to endorse any particular notion of indicative planning, but to emphasise that, whilst accepting Hayek's emphasis on the importance of the economy's means of generating and deploying information, we can reject both his formulation of the problem and the extreme political conclusions he draws from it.

The idea that socialists should not reject markets wholesale does not come primarily from the influence of Hayek. There have always been socialists who have been sceptical of the economic, but especially the political, implications of central economic planning. The significance of Hayek is the challenge he poses to examine in depth what the role of markets is, both economically and politically, and how far they are compatible with socialist objectives.

This involves rejecting the notion of market socialism, in so far as that term suggests viewing 'the market' as a principle, as both Hayek and orthodox Marxists do. Rather, the question should be how far can markets serve traditional socialist objectives. This raises issues which cannot appropriately be even sketched here, but one or two broad points may be made which are closely tied to some of Hayek's arguments.

First, as noted in Chapter 2 above, Hayek's argument for severalty of property, and its implications of the *political* desirability of labour markets, is not perhaps widely controversial on the Left. But of course the implications of markets in labour for egalitarian objectives is deeply problematic. The important general point to make is that the empirical evidence on the relation between labour markets and income distribution exemplifies the unhelpfulness of overgeneralising about the effects of markets. The existence of a market in labour in, say, Sweden is compatible with a much greater degree of equality of income than in other countries with such a market – for example, the USA (Morrisson, 1984). A range of labour-market policies (not least a very strong commitment to full employment) has enabled Sweden to combine vital freedoms in the labour market whilst at the same time restricting discriminatory practices, providing high levels of skill training, and reducing income differentials.

Second, socialists in pursuit of any kind of industrial democracy must radically reshape capital markets. But here again there is a need to distinguish among different kinds of capital market – between the extreme cases of arm's length and irresponsible capital markets, as in the USA and the UK, and the provision of funding via co-operative bodies which also provide other services to, and monitor the activities of, lending firms, as in Mondragon (Thomas and Logan, 1982, ch. 4).

Third, the key player in most markets is the large corporation. Here the scope for achieving public-policy objectives requires a radical re-shaping of how these bodies function. The question is not just the regime of regulation these enterprises are subject to, though that is plainly a much more important issue than the long debated issue of legal ownership. But beyond regulation there is a need for a radical rethink of the legal framework of the corporation. As Hayek rightly argues from his liberal perspective, the legal form of 'private property' matters – to describe property as private by itself tells us remarkably little of how it functions. From a democratic socialist point of view, exactly the same kind of point can be made.

The starting point for any such programme of change is a recognition that the modern private corporation is a creation of the public power – that the right to limited liability is a privilege granted by the law, without which few large corporations could survive. As Hirst (1989, pp. 209–10) emphasises, the original idea of limited liability was that it would be granted to companies as 'democratic republics of shareholders'. But this, of course, they no longer are. They are largely self-perpetuating oligarchies in which the shareholders (now mainly institutions) rarely intervene. What is needed, then, is to re-create the idea of the company as a democracy, but one with a variety of constituents – shareholders, employees, consumers and the community generally. The obvious pattern might be the common Continental model of a two-tier supervisory and managerial board in the company, the former being the democratic forum, making the strategic and broad policy decisions.

The argument is not that this should be the only kind of company. The case should be made for a plurality of types – for example, co-operatives (Estrin, 1989) and public mutual companies (Hirst, 1989, ch. 6) – as well as radically reformed 'ordinary' companies. But the crucial point is to attack at its root the issue of unaccountable economic power in the private corporation. This would, in turn, make much more tolerable the degree of autonomy granted to the enterprise as a result of abandoning the fantasy of subordinating their every action to some central plan, and embracing (albeit in a qualified way) markets as a way of allocating resources.

These examples merely illustrate where the arguments might begin once we leave behind the polarity of 'the market versus the plan' which Hayek's work embodies. Obviously, this polarity has been challenged before – recent examples include the work of Nove (1983), which is a fine example of learning from both Eastern Europe experience and economic theory about the limits of economic planning, without falling into the trap of counterposing the 'failure of planning' with the 'success of the market'. This point is perhaps particularly important now, when the retreat from central planning in the Soviet Union and the rest of Eastern Europe is providing an opening for Western European and American neoliberalism, including the work of Hayek, in contexts where an uncontrolled release of 'market forces' is likely to lead to disaster.

Notes

1. This approach owes a great deal to the work of Foucault – e.g. 1977, 1980. For discussion see, for example, Miller (1987) and Rose (1985).
2. I owe this formulation to Paul Hirst (1986, pp. 108–9).
3. Hayek's other objection is on the grounds that 'effective participation in the direction of an enterprise is a full-time job', an objection which not only begs a number of questions, but also lacks the ramifications of the objection discussed above.
4. For public expenditure trends in the 1980s see, for example, Henderson (1989, pp. 75–82).

Bibliography

Auerbach, P. (1988): *Competition: The Economics of Industrial Change* (Oxford: Blackwell).

Auerbach, P., Desai, M., Shamsavari, A. (1988): 'The Transition from Actually Existing Capitalism', *New Left Review* no. 170.

BSA (British Social Attitudes) (1989): *British Social Attitudes: Special International Report* (London: Gower).

Barnett, C. (1985): *The Audit of War* (London: Weidenfeld and Nicolson).

Barr, N. (1988): *Evidence* in Fifth Report of Social Services Committee Memoranda, House of Commons Paper 1987/8, 264 IV.

Barry, N. (1979): *Hayek's Social and Economic Philosophy* (London: Macmillan).

Barry, N. (1987): *The New Right* (London: Croom Helm).

Bean, C., Layard, R., Nickell, S. (1986): 'The Rise in Unemployment: A Multi-Country Study', *Economica*, vol. 53, Supplement.

Belsey, A. (1986): 'The New Right, Social Order and Civil Liberties' in R. Levitas (ed), *The Ideology of the New Right* (Cambridge: Polity).

Bergson, A. (1967): 'Market Socialism Revisited', *Journal of Political Economy*, vol. 75, no. 2.

Berlin, I. (1958): *Two Concepts of Liberty* (Oxford: Oxford University Press).

Blanchflower, D. (1986): 'What Effect do Unions Have on Relative Wages in Great Britain?, *British Journal of Industrial Relations*, vol. 24, no. 2.

Blaug, M. (1985): *Economic Theory in Retrospect* (Cambridge: Cambridge University Press), 3rd edn.

Bolton (1971): *Report of the Committee of Inquiry on Small Firms*, Command Paper 4811 (London: HMSO).

Booth, A. (1989): *British Economic Policy 1931–49: Was There a Keynesian Revolution?* (Hemel Hempstead: Wheatsheaf).

Bosanquet, N. (1983): *After the New Right* (London: Heinemann).

Brown, A.J. (1985): *World Inflation Since 1950* (Cambridge: Cambridge University Press).

Brus, W. (1972): *The Market in a Socialist Economy* (London: Routledge & Kegan Paul).
Brus, W. (1975): *Socialist Ownership and Political Systems* (London: Routledge & Kegan Paul).
Brutzkus, B. (1935): *Economic Planning in Soviet Russia* (London: Routledge & Kegan Paul).
Buchanan, J.M. (ed), (1978a): *The Economics of Politics* (London: Institute of Economic Affairs).
Buchanan, J.M., Wagner, R.E. (1977): *Democracy in Deficit* (London: Academic Press).
Buchanan, J.M., Wagner, R.E., Burton, J. (1978b): *The Consequences of Mr Keynes* (London: Institute of Economic Affairs).
Burke, E. (1790/1968): *Reflections on the Revolution in France* (ed by Conor Cruise O'Brien), (Harmondsworth: Penguin).
Burton, J. (ed), (1984): *Hayek's Serfdom Revisited* (London: Institute of Economic Affairs).
Caldwell, B.J. (1988): 'Hayek's Transformation', *History of Political Economy*, vol. 20, no. 4.
Cameron, D.R. (1984): 'Social Democracy, Corporatism, Labour Quiescence, and the Representation of Economic Interest in Advanced Capitalist Society' in J.H. Goldthorpe (ed), *Order and Conflict in Contemporary Capitalism* (Oxford: Oxford University Press).
Cave, M. (1980): *Computers and Economic Planning – The Soviet Experience* (Cambridge: Cambridge University Press).
Command Paper 7615 (1979): *Royal Commission on the National Health Service: Report* (London: HMSO).
Congdon, T. (1981): 'Is the Provision of a Sound Currency a Necessary Function of the State?', *National Westminster Bank Quarterly Review*, August.
Crafts, N. (1988): 'The Assessment: British Economic Growth over the Long Run', *Oxford Review of Economic Policy*, vol. 4, no. 1.
Crick, B. (1987): *Socialism* (Milton Keynes: Open University Press).
Cross, R. (ed) (1988): *Hysteresis and the Natural Rate Hypothesis* (Oxford: Blackwell).
Cutler, T., Williams, K., Williams, J. (1986): *Keynes, Beveridge and Beyond* (London: Routledge & Kegan Paul).
Department of Employment (1990): 'Industrial Disputes: Causes', *Department of Employment Gazette*, March.
DHSS (1976): *Priorities for Health and Personal Social Services in England* (London: HMSO).
Dicey, A.V. (1914): *Lectures on the Relation Between Law and Public Opinion in England During the Nineteenth Century*, 2nd edn (London: Macmillan).
Dickinson, H.D. (1939): *Economics of Socialism* (Oxford: Oxford University Press).

Donzelot, J. (1980): *The Policing of Families* (London: Hutchinson).
Dostaler, G., Ethier, D. (1989): *Friedrich Hayek: Philosophie, économie et politique* (Paris: Economica).
Dow, S. (1985): *Macroeconomic Thought* (Oxford: Blackwell).
Downs, A. (1957): *An Economic Theory of Democracy* (New York: Harper and Row).
Downs, A. (1960): 'Why the Government Budget is Too Small in a Democracy', *World Politics*, vol. 12, no. 4.
Durbin, E. (1985): *New Jerusalems* (London: Routledge & Kegan Paul).
Elster, J. (1985): *Making Sense of Marx* (Cambridge: Cambridge University Press).
Estrin, S. (1989): 'Workers' Co-operatives: Their Merits and Their Limitations' in J. Le Grand and S. Estrin (eds), *Market Socialism* (Oxford: Oxford University Press).
Estrin, S., Winter, D. (1989): 'Planing in a Market Socialist Economy' in Le Grand, J., Estrin, S. (eds), *Market Socialism* (Oxford: Oxford University Press).
Finer, H.E. (1946): *The Road to Reaction* (New York: Dennis Dobson).
Forbes, I. (ed) (1987): *Market Socialism: Whose Choice?* (London: Fabian Society).
Foster, J. (1976): 'The Redistributive Effect of Inflation on Building Society Shares and Deposits 1961–74', *Bulletin of Economic Research*, vol. 28, no. 2.
Foucault, M. (1977): *Discipline and Punish* (London: Allen Lane).
Foucault, M. (1980): 'Two Lectures' in *Power/Knowledge*, ed. C. Gordon (Brighton: Harvester).
Freeman, R., Medoff, J. (1984): *What Do Unions Do?* (New York: Basic Books).
Freud, S. (1930): *Civilisation and its Discontents, Collected Works*, vol. 21, (London: Hogarth Press).
Friedman, D. (1985): *The Misunderstood Miracle* (Ithaca, New York: Cornell University Press).
Friedman, M. (1977): 'Inflation and Unemployment', *Journal of Political Economy*, vol. 85, no. 3.
Galbraith, J.K. (1958): *The Affluent Society* (Harmondsworth: Penguin).
Gamble, A. (1988): *The Free Economy and the Strong State: The Politics of Thatcherism* (London: Macmillan).
Geras, N. (1985): 'The Controversy about Marx and Justice', *New Left Review*, no. 150.
Gissurarson, H.H. (1987): *Hayek's Conservative Liberalism* (New York: Garland).
Goodin, R.E. (1985): 'Self-Reliance versus the Welfare State', *Journal of Social Policy*, vol. 14, no. 1.
Gray, J. (1984): *Hayek on Liberty* (Oxford: Blackwell).
Gray, J. (1988): 'F.A. von Hayek' in R. Scruton (ed), *Conservative Thinkers: Essays from the Salisbury Review* (London: Claridge Press).

Hall, P. (1986): *Governing the Economy* (Cambridge: Polity).
Hammermesh, D.S., Rees, A. (1988): *The Economics of Work and Pay*, 4th edn (New York: Harper and Row).
Harden, I., Lewis, N. (1986): *The Noble Lie: The British Constitution and the Rule of Law* (London: Hutchinson).
Hare, P. (1985): *Planning the British Economy* (London: Macmillan).
Harrod, R. (1946): 'Professor Hayek on Liberalism', *Economic Journal*, vol. 56, no. 3.
Heald, D. (1983): *Public Expenditure: Its Defence and Reform* (Oxford: Martin Robertson).
Henderson, D. (1989): 'A New Age of Reform?', *Fiscal Studies*, vol. 10, no. 3.
Hicks, J. (1967): *Critical Essays in Monetary Theory* (Oxford: Oxford University Press).
Hills, J. (1988): *Changing Tax: How the Tax System Works and How to Change It* (London: Child Poverty Action Group).
Hindess, B. (1983): *Parliamentary Democracy and Socialist Politics* (London: Routledge & Kegan Paul).
Hindess, B. (1987): *Freedom, Equality and the Market* (London: Tavistock).
Hindess, B. (1988): *Choice, Rationality and Social Theory* (London: Unwin Hyman).
Hirschman, A.O. (1977): *The Passions and the Interests* (Princeton, New Jersey: Princeton University Press).
Hirschman, A.O. (1982): *Shifting Involvements: Private Interest and Public Interest* (Oxford: Martin Robertson).
Hirst, P. (1985): 'Socialism, Pluralism, and Law', *International Journal of the Sociology of Law*, vol. 13, no. 2.
Hirst, P. (1986): *Law, Socialism and Democracy* (London: Allen & Unwin).
Hirst, P. (1987): 'Carl Schmitt's Decisionism', *Telos*, no. 72.
Hirst, P. (1989): *After Thatcher* (London: Collins).
Hirst, P., Woolley, P. (1982): *Social Relations and Human Attributes* (London: Tavistock).
Hirst, P., Zeitlin, J. (1989): 'Flexible Specialisation and the Competitive Failure of UK Manufacturing', *Political Quarterly*, vol. 60, no. 2.
Hodgson, G. (1984): *The Democratic Economy* (Harmondsworth: Penguin).
Hodgson, G. (1988): *Economics and Institutions* (Cambridge: Polity).
Hume, D. (1738/1968): *A Treatise of Human Nature* (London: Dent).
Hutchison, T.W. (1981): *The Politics and Philosophy of Economics* (Oxford: Blackwell).
Johnson, C. (1982): *MITI and the Japanese Miracle* (Stanford, Conn: Stanford University Press).
Kaldor, N. (1939): 'Capital Intensity and the Trade Cycle', *Economica*, vol. 6, no. 2.

Kaldor, N. (1942): 'Professor Hayek and the Concertina Effect', *Economica*, vol. 9, no. 4.
Kant, I. (1781/1934): *Critique of Pure Reason*, trans. J.M.D Meiklejohn (London: Dent).
Keynes, J.M. (1923/1971): *A Tract on Monetary Reform, Collected Writings*, vol. 4 (London: Macmillan).
Keynes, J.M. (1930/1971): *A Treatise on Money: Collected Writings*, vols. 5, 6 (London: Macmillan).
Keynes, J.M. (1931/1973): 'The Pure Theory of Money: A Reply to Dr Hayek' in *The General Theory and After: Part 1, Preparation, Collected Writings*, vol. 13 (London: Macmillan).
Keynes, J.M. (1936/1973): *The General Theory of Employment, Interest and Money* (London: Macmillan).
Keynes, J.M. (1944/1980): *Activities 1940–46, Shaping the Post-War World Employment and Commodities: Collected Writings*, vol. 27 (London: Macmillan).
Keynes, J.M. (1945/1980): *Activities 1940–46, Shaping the Post-War World Employment and Commodities: Collected Writings*, vol. 27 (London: Macmillan).
Klein, R. (1983): *The Politics of the NHS* (London: Longman).
Kornai, J. (1971): *Anti-Equilibrium*, (London: North Holland).
Kristol, I. (1971): 'When Virtue Loses all her Loveliness' in D. Bell and I. Kristol, *Capitalism Today* (New York: Basic Books).
Kukathas, C. (1989): *Hayek and Modern Liberalism* (Oxford: Oxford University Press).
Lange, O., Taylor, F.M. (1938): *On the Economic Theory of Socialism* ed. B. Lippincott (New York: McGraw-Hill).
Lavoie, D. (1985): *Rivalry and Central Planning: The Socialist Calculation Debate Reconsidered* (Cambridge: Cambridge University Press).
Layard, R., Nickell, S. (1986): 'Unemployment in Britain', *Economica*, vol. 53, Supplement.
Layard, R., Nickell, S. (1987): *An Incomes Policy to Help the Unemployed* (London: Employment Institute).
Le Grand, J. (1982): *The Strategy of Equality* (London: Allen & Unwin).
Le Grand, J. (1989): 'Markets, Welfare and Equality' in Le Grand, J., Estrin, S. (eds) *Market Socialism* (Oxford University Press).
Leathers, C.G. (1989): 'Scotland's New Poll Taxes as Hayekian Policy', *Scottish Journal of Political Economy*, vol. 36, no. 2.
Lindblom, C. (1977): *Politics and Markets* (New York: Basic Books).
Machlup, F. (1974): 'F. von Hayek's Contribution to Economics', *Swedish Journal of Economics*, vol. 76, no. 4.
Machlup, F. (ed), (1977): *Essays on Hayek* (London: Routledge & Kegan Paul).
Machlup, F. (1979): 'F.A. Hayek' in *International Encyclopaedia of the Social Sciences*, vol. 18 (New York: Free Press).

Mandel, E. (1986): 'In Defence of Socialist Planning', *New Left Review* no. 159.
Matthews, R.C.O. (1968): 'Why Has Britain Had Full Employment Since the War?', *Economic Journal*, vol. 78, no. 2.
Maynard, G., van Ryckeghem, W. (1976): *A World of Inflation* (London: Batsford).
McCloughry, R. (ed), (1984): *Money, Capital and Fluctuations: Early Essays* (London: Routledge & Kegan Paul).
Mill, J.S. (1896): *Principles of Political Economy*, 6th ed. (London: Longmans, Green & Co.)
Mill, J.S. (1859/1962): 'On "Liberty"' in M. Warnock (ed), *Utilitarianism* (London: Fontana).
Miller, P. (1987): *Domination and Power* (London: Routledge & Kegan Paul).
Minson, J. (1985): *Genealogies of Morals: Nietzsche, Foucault, Donzelot and the Eccentricity of Morals* (London: Macmillan).
Minson, J. (1989): 'Men and Manners: "Kantian Humanism", Rhetoric and the History of Ethics', *Economy and Society*, vol. 18, no. 2.
Morrisson, C. (1984): 'Income Distribution in Eastern Europe and Western Countries', *Journal of Comparative Economics*, vol. 8, no. 2.
Nash, G.H. (1976): *The Conservative Intellectual Movement in America Since 1945* (New York: Basic Books).
Newell, A., Symons, J.S.V. (1986): *Corporatism, the Laissez-Faire and the Rise in Unemployment* (London: LSE Centre for Labour Economics), Discussion Paper no. 260.
Nishiyama, C., Leube, K.R. (1984): *The Essence of Hayek* (Stanford, Calif.: Hoover Institution Press).
Nove, A. (1983): *The Economics of Feasible Socialism* (London: Allen & Unwin).
Oswald, A.J. (1986): 'Wage Determination and Recession', *British Journal of Industrial Relations*, vol. 24, no. 1.
Peele, G. (1984): *Revival and Reaction* (Oxford: Oxford University Press).
Plant, R. (1989): 'Socialism, Markets, and End States' in J. Le Grand, S. Estrin (eds), *Market Socialism* (Oxford: Oxford University Press).
Polanyi, K. (1944): *The Great Transformation* (London: Gollancz).
Polanyi-Levitt, K., Mendell, M. (1989): 'The Origins of Market Fetishism', *Monthly Review*, vol. 40, no. 6.
Popper, K. (1959): *The Logic of Scientific Discovery* (London: Hutchinson; first published in German, in 1934).
Robbins, L. (1934): *The Great Depression* (London: Macmillan).
Robbins, L. (1935): *An Essay on the Nature and Significance of Economic Science*, 2nd edn (London: Macmillan).
Robbins, L. (1961): 'Hayek on Liberty', *Economica*, vol. 28, no. 1.
Robbins, L. (1971): *Autobiography of an Economist* (London: Macmillan).

Roll, E. (1945): Review of Hayek's *Road to Serfdom*, *American Economic Review*, vol. 35, no. 1.
Rose, N. (1985): *The Psychological Complex: Psychology, Politics and Society in England 1869–1939* (London: Routledge & Kegan Paul).
Sahlins, M. (1974): *Stone Age Economics* (London: Tavistock).
Scherer, F.M. (1980): *Industrial Market Structure and Economic Performance*, 2nd edn (Chicago: Rand McNally).
Schumpeter, J. (1942): *Capitalism, Socialism and Democracy* (London: Allen & Unwin).
Schumpeter, J. (1952): *Ten Great Economists* (London: Allen & Unwin).
Shackle, G.L. (1981): 'F.A. Hayek' in D.P. O'Brien, J.R. Presley (eds), *Pioneering Modern Economics in Britain* (London: Macmillan).
Shand, A.H. (1984): *The Capitalist Alternative: An Introduction to Neo-Austrian Economics* (Brighton: Wheatsheaf).
Skidelsky, R. (1983): *John Maynard Keynes: Hopes Betrayed 1883–1920* (London: Macmillan).
Smith, A. (1776/1976): *The Wealth of Nations*, ed. R.H. Campbell and A.S. Skinner (Oxford: Oxford University Press).
Sraffa, P. (1932): 'Dr Hayek on Money and Capital', *Economic Journal*, vol. 42, no. 1.
Talmon, J.L. (1952): *The Origins of Totalitarian Democracy* (London: Secker and Warburg).
Taylor-Gooby, P. (1985): *Public Opinion, Ideology and State Welfare* (London: Routledge & Kegan Paul).
Therborn, G. (1986): *Why Some Peoples Are More Unemployed than Others* (London: Verso).
Thomas, H., Logan, C. (1982): *Mondragon: An Economic Analysis* (London: Allen & Unwin).
Thompson, E.P. (1963): *The Making of the English Working Class* (London: Gollancz).
Thompson, E.P. (1975): *Whigs and Hunters: Origin of the Black Act* (London: Allen Lane).
Tomlinson, J. (1981): 'The Economics of Politics and Public Expenditure: A Critique', *Economy and Society*, vol. 10, no. 4.
Tomlinson, J. (1987): *Employment Policy: The Crucial Years 1939–1955* (Oxford: Oxford University Press).
Tomlinson, J. (1990): *Public Policy and the Economy Since 1900* (Oxford: Oxford University Press).
Toye, J.F.J. (1976): 'Economic Theories of Politics and Public Finance', *British Journal of Political Science*, vol. 6, no. 4.
UN (1987): *National Account Statistics: Analysis of Main Aggregates 1983/84* (New York: UN).
Wadhwani, S. (1986): 'Inflation, Bankruptcy, Default Premia and the Stock Market', *Economic Journal*, vol. 96, no. 1.
Wadhwani, S. (1987): 'Effects of Inflation on Real Wages and Employment', *Economica*, vol. 54, no. 1.

Wedderburn, W. (1989): 'Freedom of Association and Philosophies of Labour Law', *Industrial Law Journal*, vol. 18, no. 1.

Wilczynski, J. (1970): *The Economics of Socialism* (London: Allen & Unwin).

● Williams, K. (1975): 'Facing Reality: A Critique of Karl Popper's Empiricism', *Economy and Society*, vol. 4, no. 3.

Williams, K., Williams, J., Thomas, D. (1983): *Why Are the British Bad at Manufacturing?* (London: Routledge & Kegan Paul).

Wilson, T., Wilson D.J. (1982): *Political Economy of the Welfare State* (London: Allen & Unwin).

Wootton, B. (1945): *Freedom Under Planning* (London: Allen & Unwin).

Wright, A. (1986): *Socialisms: Theories and Practices* (Oxford: Oxford University Press).

Index

altruism 22, 24, 44, 57, 58, 60, 143
Austrian economics 1, 6, 16, 109–10, 113, 127–8

Barry, Brian xi, 50, 54, 60
Bentham, Jeremy 32
Blaug, Mark 6
Bretton Woods 70, 77
Brutzkus, B. 103
Burke, Edmund 27, 52, 55

Capitalism and the Historians 46
Chicago, University of 11, 12
Choice in Currency 15
Cole, G.D.H. 117, 137
collectivism 46, 49, 51, 96, 116, 124
Collectivist Economic Planning 7–8, 9, 102, 103, 104, 115, 118
competition 23, 24, 60, 62
Condorcet, M. 52
Congdon, Tim 50, 79–80
conservatism viii–ix, 25, 37, 42, 52, 55, 56, 61, 64–5, 130, 143
constitution 14–15, 26–7, 28, 29, 138
The Constitution of Liberty x, 13, 18, 19, 20, 21, 24, 25, 26, 27, 31, 44, 46, 53, 54, 62, 64, 67, 80–1, 82–3, 84, 88, 90, 95–6, 114, 119, 128, 134–5, 139

co-operation 23, 57, 61, 143–5
co-operative firms 25, 120, 144, 149
corporations 91, 94–5, 120–1, 124, 131, 135–6, 141, 149–50
The Counter-Revolution of Science 10, 126
Crick, Bernard 137, 139

democracy 25–31, 134–40
 industrial 28, 94–5, 135–6, 149, 151
Denationalisation of Money 15, 31, 50, 79
Descartes, René 45
Dow, Sheila 126–7, 127–8
Downs, Anthony 73–4

economic calculation 100–15
Economic Freedom and Representative Government 14, 26
economic planning 7, 102–4, 106–11, 114–5, 117–9, 144, 146, 147, 148
Economics and Knowledge 8
entrepreneur 105, 112–13
epistemology 12, 27
equality 22–3, 24, 41–2, 80–5, 140–2
Estrin, Saul 142
evolution ix, 32, 34, 42–52
 Darwinian 42–3, 65
family 130–2, 133

The Fatal Conceit: The Errors of Socialism 4–5, 7, 15, 39, 43, 45, 46, 47, 51, 57, 58, 62, 100, 122–3
feminism 56–7
Ferguson, Adam 52
France x, 121
fraternity 143–5
freedom 18–27, 96–9
  'negative' 20, 22, 128–9, 130
  'positive' 20, 22, 130–1
  see also liberty
Freiburg, University of 13
Freud, Sigmund 51–2
Friedman, Milton 69, 70, 99
full employment 68–80, 92, 93
Full Employment at Any Price? 14

Galbraith, J.K. 123
General Theory of Employment, Interest and Money 4

Hicks, John 4
Hirschman, A.O. 51
Hirst, Paul 29, 149–50, 151
Hodgson, Geoff 108, 110, 120, 125
Hume, David 31, 38, 52, 57, 65, 66

income distribution 39–40, 60, 83, 141
incomes policies 77–8
Individualism and Economic Order 8, 101, 103, 105, 106, 126, 147
inflation 68–80, 89, 93–4
interest groups 29–30
Institute of Economic Affairs 12
invisible hand 32, 113–14

John Stuart Mill and Harriet Taylor 11
justice 38–42
  social 38–40, 80–1, 82–3, 140–1
Kaldor, Nikolas 6

Kant, Immanuel 10, 12, 64, 65
Keynes, J.M. 2, 3, 16, 51, 68–70, 74, 76, 124
Keynesianism viii, 5–6, 68, 74–5, 76, 99
Klein, Rudolph 87
knowledge 8

laissez-faire viii, 7
Lavoie, D. 108–9
law 31–8
  common 33, 36
  private 33, 38
  public 36
  see also rule of law
Law, Legislation and Liberty x, 14, 19, 20, 25, 26, 31, 32, 33, 38, 40, 43, 45, 46, 47, 51, 52, 53, 54, 58, 61, 88, 89, 91, 141, 142
liberalism viii, 17–18, 64–5, 98, 133
libertarianism x, 51, 133
liberty 17–25, 117, 128–34, 135, 139–40
London School of Economics 2, 6

majority rule 26, 28
Mandel, Ernest 146
market socialism 108, 145–50
markets xi–xii, 8, 39, 57, 58, 60, 102, 106–11, 119–21, 127, 140–1, 147–8, 150
  see also spontaneous order
Marxism 35, 48, 52, 56, 66, 101, 107, 134, 143, 146, 148
Matthews, R.C.O. 76
Menger, Carl 1
Mill, John Stuart 11, 19
Mises, von 1, 2, 102, 108
Monetary Theory and the Trade Cycle 5
Mont Pelerin Society 1
Montesquieu, C. 47, 48
morals 57–63
Myrdal, Gunnar 13

National Health Service 82, 85–7
neo-classical economics 8, 109, 110, 120, 125

New Right viii, x, 145
  American ix, x
New Studies in Philosophy, Politics, Economics and the History of Ideas 4, 59, 67, 68, 69–71, 72–3
Nobel Prize 13
Nove, Alec 107, 150

On Liberty 12

parliamentary democracy 30, 36–7, 137–8
pensions 81–2, 84–5
physiocrats 52
Popper, Karl 10, 51, 126
population growth 49, 57–8, 123, 128
Prices and Production 2, 5, 68, 127
private property ix, 17, 24–5, 29, 31, 44, 45, 57, 102–3, 104
Profits, Interest and Investment 5
public borrowing 75–6
public choice 73–5, 76
public expenditure 75–6
The Pure Theory of Capital 6

rationalism 27, 32, 45–6, 54, 56
Reagan, Ronald x, 141
reason 27, 30, 52–7
The Road to Serfdom ix, xi, 4, 10–11, 18, 115–21
Robbins, Lionel 3, 4
Ricardo Effect 5
Rousseau, Jean-Jacques 45–6, 52
rule of law 18, 32–3, 34–7, 91
rules of conduct 18, 19, 38, 48, 59–60, 144

Schumpeter, Joseph 101, 108, 109, 123, 143

scientism 10, 69
The Sensory Order 12
small business 97–8
Smith, Adam 22, 23, 48, 52, 114
socialism 7, 9–10, 15, 22, 23, 25, 51, 60, 100–23, 145–50
  see also market socialism
social insurance 81–2, 83–4
spontaneous order 20, 22, 23, 39
  see also markets
Sraffa, Piero 3
states 132–3
Studies in Philosophy, Politics and Economics 8, 11, 39, 44, 91
subjectivism 8, 110–11, 126–7
Sweden 149

Talmon, J.L. 56
Thatcher, Margaret x–xi, 78, 135, 141
Thompson, E.P. 35
A Tiger by the Tail 4, 14
totalitarianism 26, 70
Trade Disputes Act (1906) 88, 90–1
Trade Union Act (1871) 90
trade unions 87–96, 131
tradition 46, 48, 54–5, 56–7, 133–4
Treatise on Money 2
Trotsky, Leon 25

USA ix, x, 1, 11, 12, 87, 135, 141, 149
1980s Unemployment and the Unions 4, 14, 88, 89–90

Webb, B. & S. 117
Welfare State 59, 63, 80–7, 96–7, 123
Wells, H.G. 117
West Germany x, 77
Wieser, von 1
Wootton, Barbara xi, 21, 96, 130